UMI Publications, In

March 26, 2001

Dear Race Fan,

We are proud to present Bill's new book; Bill Elliott: The Fan's Favorite. We at UMI fully realize you have been waiting patiently for this book. First of all, we sincerely apologize for the tardiness of this book. Everyone at Bill Elliott Racing and here at UMI wanted this book to be as near perfect as possible and we hope you feel it was worth the wait.

As a gesture to thank you for your patience, we have included a FREE copy of the OFFICIAL NASCAR PREVIEW AND PRESS GUIDE. We hope you find it useful during the 2001 NASCAR Winston Cup Season.

We, UMI Publications, Inc., know how loyal NASCAR fan's are to their favorite sport. We will make every attempt to earn and keep your support. You, the NASCAR fan, are the backbone of this sport. Once again, we sincerely apologize for keeping you waiting. Please enjoy!!!!

UMI Publications, Inc.

Bill Elliott ®

THE
FANS' FAVORITE

Acknowledgments

UMI Publications is proud to present *Bill Elliott: The Fan's Favorite*. Producing this book was a challenging and rewarding project for us. To ensure that every aspect of this book was as near perfect as possible, many people took extra time out of their already full schedules to help. We would like to take a moment to extend thanks to everyone involved.

First our deepest thanks go out to Bill and Cindy Elliott for giving us this opportunity. Between a busy race schedule, appearances, and business to run, both Bill and Cindy found time for interviews, photo selection, and reviews. Without their help and guidance none of this would have been possible. In addition to Bill and Cindy, we would also like to thank all Elliott family members for their assistance. We would also like to thank Mrs. Judy Moss for all her help in locating everything we asked for from photos to scheduling interview times. Although they are too many to name, we wish to thank all the dedicated employees at Bill Elliott Racing and all his sponsors.

Special thanks also go out to all our friends at NASCAR including Mr. Bill France, Mr. Jim France, Mr. Brian France, Lesa Kennedy, Mr. Paul Brooks, Mr. George Pyne, Ms. Kelley Crouch, Ms. Jennifer White, Mr. John Griffin, and Mr. Paul Schaffer.

Ben Blake wrote this book. Ben probably had the hardest assignment of anyone. Putting Bill's career into words was no easy task and we extend thanks to Ben for the countless hours he put into this project.

The photography included in this book is the best available. Special thanks go to all the photographers that contributed images for consideration, including Mrs. Cindy Elliott, Mr. David Chobat, Mr. Ernie Masche, Mr. Don Grassman, Mr. Larry Foster, Mr. Dozier Mobley, Mr. Keith Smith, Mr. Elmer Kappell, Mr. Garry Eller, and Cameras in Action Stock Photograhy, Inc. Extra special thanks have to go to Bill and Cindy for allowing us access to their private family albums. Also, special thanks are extended to Mr. Garry Hill for allowing us to reprint his legendary "Pass in the Grass."

Finally, the most sincere thanks go out to you—the fans. It is you that have made Bill's career so successful. This book is especially for you with our thanks. Thank you again for all your support over the years.

PRESIDENT AND PUBLISHER
Ivan Mothershead

VICE PRESIDENT AND ASSOCIATE PUBLISHER
Charlie Keiger

VICE PRESIDENT
Rick Peters

CONTROLLER
Lewis Patton

NATIONAL ADVERTISING MANAGER
Mark Cantey

ADVERTISING ACCOUNT EXECUTIVE
Paul Kaperoris

MANAGING EDITOR
Ward Woodbury

SENIOR EDITOR
Nat Walker

ART DIRECTOR
Brett Shippy

SENIOR DESIGNERS
Rainbow Graphics
Edgar Bowery
David Hommel

MANAGER OF INFORMATION SYSTEMS
Chris Devera

CUSTOMER SERVICE REPRESENTATIVES
Mary Flowe, Carla Greene,
Heather Guy, Joanie Tarbert

Foreword by Bill Elliott

"How do you repay the person for being such a fan to you over the years? I'm at a loss sometimes. You wish there was some way you could do things for them. You hope that maybe you have in certain ways."

As Bill Elliott completed his 25th season in racing, he felt obliged to those who have given him unwavering support throughout his career. What follows is an open letter from Bill to his fans.

"I think it's been more family-driven, more so than singling me out. I think people could relate to us. We came in kind of like a David-and-Goliath deal. We weren't a Petty or a Yarborough or a name that was recognized. We were a small family team just trying to race, and for that to happen today would be impossible.

"I think the family—Mother and Daddy and what they were doing, all the people they touched through the years, my grandmother—I think we were able to relate to a lot of people, young and old. The fan base has stuck with us through thick and thin.

"I guess what I'm trying to say is *they've* kept it alive. It motivated me and them, as far as getting other people involved. Some fans come out here and say 'I'm a "whoever" fan,' but as far as showing any support, they don't. With my fans, if I say I'm going to go jump off this building, they'll go with me.

"It's a very unique situation. They've just been so behind me. It's just part of what they want to do. It's a challenge to them to go out and get this done, show their support."

You would think there would be some sensitivity among Ford fans, with Bill switching to Dodge in 2001 after such a long time with Ford. The Elliotts revived Ford's fortunes in the early 1980s, and many Ford fans came on board. But nothing has changed among Bill's backers.

"It's like, OK, I have to go on to something else, but there again, the fans believe in me, believe in the entirety. I have not had one fan say one negative thing to me about that. Even the diehard Ford fans say, 'We're going to miss you,' but most of them say, 'We're going to support you.'

"I think another thing that has probably helped me the last several years is that I've enjoyed the McDonald's relationship, dealing with the kids and families. This set up fit me very well. But now, I'm going to the next step, this new arrangement with everyone involved—the team, everything."

"I think I lose sight of the impact I've made on people's lives throughout my career. I have been told by some fans that I take them out of their hardship and for a while they believe that they can be Bill Elliott behind the wheel driving 200 mph—something I take for granted. I take it day-in and day-out for granted.

"I think that's the thing you look back on when you see all this stuff [in the Museum], all these things from shirts and coats and blankets, all sorts of odds and ends people have made throughout the years.

"It amazes me. It comes back to the impact you have somehow instilled in the people's minds and the loyalty they have to you throughout the years, the appreciation, whatever you want to call it.

"How do you repay them? How do you repay the person for being such a fan to you over the years? I'm at a loss sometimes. You wish there was some way you could do things for them. You hope that maybe you have in certain ways."

Contents

A Tribute

I n one respect, I kind of don't know where to start. I've been real fortunate in my life and career, and so many people have contributed that it makes it hard to name one or two, or even a hundred or a thousand.

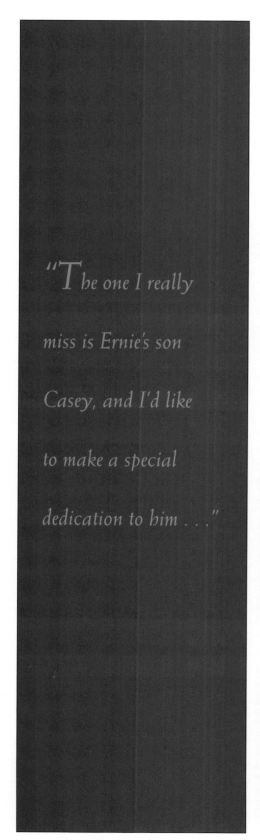

"The one I really miss is Ernie's son Casey, and I'd like to make a special dedication to him . . ."

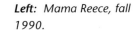

Above: George Elliott.
Left: Ernie and Casey share some free time after Casey's qualifying for the Busch Race at Darlington.
Below: Mildred Elliott and "Fluffy" the cat in front of Mama's house.

Somebody asked me who would be the first people I'd give this book to, who I would dedicate it to. Looking at it from that side, I'd have to say Mother and Daddy—Mildred Elliott and George Elliott—they were there from the beginning. Mother and Daddy sacrificed a lot in getting us where we're at. He enjoyed racing, and they always put aside what they wanted to do, putting a little bit of extra money on the racing instead of them going on a vacation together.

Mother got to see the good days of it before she passed away. I owe a lot to Daddy, but Mother sacrificed, she gave up a lot. They both worked very hard, a lot of hours. Daddy had the building supply and acquired a Ford dealership. He made a decent living, but he had to work hard to make a go of it.

Really, if you look at it, my family is the main thing. We all worked hard. That's what we were expected to do when we came in from school in the afternoon. I can look back to my Grandma, who we called Mama Reese, with as much as she did for us, she was always there for us, always a part of what was going on. I lived in her basement there for about a year, and we were all pretty close.

Coming back to Daddy's side of it, Daddy was always leading me in NASCAR's direction. I was trying to put a race car together to go out and play around. He took some of his stuff and said, 'Go race this.' He kept leading me to that NASCAR door. He realized if we were ever going to go to the next level, NASCAR was going to be the way to go. This racing organization has taken a big leap in the last 10 or 15 years compared to where it was at

back when I started in the mid '70s. Looking at the whole scheme of things, a lot of things have changed, and Grandma and Mom and Dad—all the folks—helped me through this whole deal.

You can't talk about the family without talking about my brothers, Ernie and Dan. My dad started the speed shop business in the late '60s that Ernie ended up running, and Ernie kind of led me into that. We were all real close, which really is what made it happen. Ernie was the ideal crew chief for me, because we were *family*, and he knew what the car was doing as fast as I knew what it was doing—he could *read* me. Dan, along with build-

Above: With Bill doing the driving and brothers Ernie and Dan providing great engines and strategy, this trio was one of the best in NASCAR history, keeping Bill at the front almost every weekend.

Center: Bill and brother Ernie talk strategy before a race at Charlotte in 1984.

Right: Bill and brother Dan at Daytona, 1985.

ing our transmissions, was the man who kept everyone's morale consistently pumped and the pit crew focused and well-polished for race day. He was also my tire-changer, and as you've heard so many times, it does take an entire team effort to be successful. There wasn't but a handful of us, but we all worked together at it.

Right: Starr was the apple of her daddy's eye, especially when she congratulated him in victory lane!
Below: Chase gets a firsthand look at the inside of his dad's "office."

The ones I really have come to appreciate are the ones in my own family, my wife Cindy, my son Chase, and our daughters Brittany and Starr. I realized, when I was able to put all that together and make it work, how important that is to your life. In the '80s, all I cared about was racing, 100 percent, run wide-open as hard as I could go and never look back. It doesn't have to be that way; there's time for your family.

The sad part is that Mother and Daddy can't be around with us together. The one I really miss is Ernie's son Casey, and I'd like to make a special dedication to him because he had so much to live for. It's just sad that Casey was not able to continue on. That's just an unfortunate part of life. You're here for a short spell of time, and you don't know when the end's going to be. He and I were as close as brothers. He never had anything bad to say about anybody, he never got into anything, and he was always a good kid. He had a future as far as racing was concerned. As he came on, he went on up the ladder with Ernie, and he never was intimidated by it at all. We all knew he could do it.

Left: Casey Elliott loved fly-fishing. It was a favorite pastime.

Above: Three generations of Elliotts. Ernie (left) and George help Casey celebrate after a race victory.

The more I think about it, the more people come to mind. You go back to the guys who helped when we started in Dawsonville—Ricky Wilson, Scotty Gaddis, Michael Hill—they were the very first guys who helped out on the team. Some of them weren't able to carry on to the next level. Chuck Hill got hurt so bad at Riverside, then we lost Mike Rich at Atlanta. But all those guys, if I'd say we were going to jump off a building, they'd be right there and say *let's go.*

There's no way you can thank everybody—Benny Parsons, Harry Melling, Junior Johnson, Jim and Jan Knutson in

Above: The loss of Mike Rich in November 1990 was a traumatic time for Bill and everyone else on the race team.

Bill Elliott

Michigan. The Frances—I was fortunate to know Bill Sr. for awhile, and I appreciate the grit and tenacity Bill France Jr. has got, the support they've given us throughout the years through good and bad.

The list goes on and on. I've probably met a half a million people in the time I've been racing, and every one of them, especially the fans, contributed something, whether they bring you a sandwich or a Coca-Cola or pat you on the back no matter how bad you did and say, 'Get 'em next week.'

This book may be about me, but this book is *for* you, every one of you.

Bill Elliott

Bill Elliott, 2001

Top: *Short-track race driver Jody Ridley (here with his brother, Biddle) was an early role model for Bill. In fact, Jody drove relief for Bill in the 1989 Daytona 500.*

Middle: *Elliott racing was sponsored by Mell-Gear at Atlanta in 1980. A second-place start really was "the start of something big" in seasons to come.*

Left: *Bill's first Winston Cup Series ride was this Torino his dad bought from Bobby Allison.*

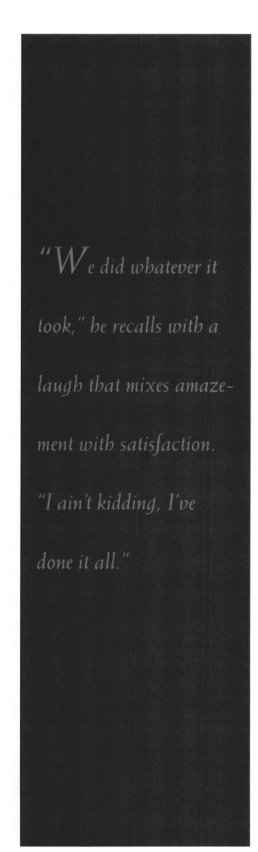

Introduction

"*We did whatever it took,*" *he recalls with a laugh that mixes amazement with satisfaction.* "*I ain't kidding, I've done it all.*"

Bill Elliott never asked for much, and certainly expected little, from racing as he grew into it during his late-teen years. Racing was the next step, a natural step, something he learned he was good at and came to enjoy, something that grew out of what his family did—which, if you listen to Bill in the pages that follow, set path, pace, and boundary for everything that came after.

If you listen carefully to Bill, or if you have over the years, you get a sense that he was dragged screaming into the big time, and once there never felt comfortable with the obligations and expectations. He's always been Bill, youngest son of George and Mildred, little brother of Ernie and Dan. And he still is—and not far from the surface.

In a lot of ways, you could say Bill grew up around racing, and then racing grew up around him. Bill Elliott and Dale Earnhardt, more than any two racers alive today, boosted NASCAR toward its modern era of flash and prosperity. The irony is that neither saw anything like this kind of light as a youngster, and both had to grow with the sport as it grew.

What sets Elliott apart—really, alone might be the better word—has been his ability to deal with what came along, shoulders-up and straightforward. Racing isn't easy, life isn't easy, and it's fair to say that no one knows that better than Bill Elliott, who grew up in that way.

Here's a kid who chipped bricks, dug ditches, drove heavy-delivery for his father's business before he had a driver's license, milked cows, helped haul parts to a dozen little racetracks around home ground, cut cylinder heads, honed bores, worked literally from sunup to past sundown. It was all in the way he was raised—all in the family.

"We did whatever it took," he recalls with a laugh that mixes amazement with satisfaction. "I ain't kidding, I've done it all."

Bill rewarded his Dad and Harry with a championship in 1988.

Bill's twenty-five years of racing has been filled with countless highs and lows, including a violent crash at Talladega and an exciting move to a new Dodge Intrepid in the 2001 season.

Bill Elliott

That's where it came from, from having his feet on the ground when he started. Through all the years, through what amounted to explosions, earthquakes, and tornadoes, that's stood him well.

Here was a kid who came out of nowhere and landed in a starburst on the racing scene in 1984. That starburst caught the racing world on fire—and caught the attention of millions—in 1985, when he pushed all of NASCAR's records skyward and launched the sport into million-dollar territory.

A million, odd to say, is routine today, but someone had to be the first to do it, and Bill was the youngster cast suddenly into the kettle and expected to grow up in a hurry, to grow from Dawsonville, Georgia, to New York and beyond, in the time it took to say Awesome Bill.

From there, what Bill had grown quietly into became a career, a phenomenon—whether he wanted it or not. NASCAR's all-time speed record. The Winston Cup in 1988. A glamour ride with Junior Johnson and Budweiser in the early 1990s. The high expectations of his self-launch with McDonalds in 1994. His perpetual popularity, what with fans voting him their favorite year after year.

In between came crashes, broken bones, deaths, divorce, and loss—losses of loved ones and friends, unavoidable things that happens to every family came down the turnpike and had to be handled. It's safe to say that few have handled racing, and life, better than Bill Elliott has, all on his own even keel.

Just let him be, and he'll figure out how to handle it all. He's built that way, made up that way.

This book comes about for a couple of reasons. First, Bill is completing 25 seasons in racing in March 2001—he started his Winston Cup career in the fall race at Rockingham, North Carolina, in 1975, and a monarch, even a reluctant one, deserves commemoration. It's hard to believe, isn't it, that Bill Elliott, the great comet of racing in the 1980s, has been with us for a quarter of a century. Good gosh, time goes by!

Second, Bill and wife Cindy want to let you know a little more of what you've seen only in newspapers and magazines—the man Bill Elliott, and all of what makes him what he is today, which really, honestly, isn't that much different from what he was as a kid 25 years ago.

He's seen a lot, and he's endured a lot, but deep down he hasn't changed a bit. Forget all the business about Awesome Bill from Dawsonville.

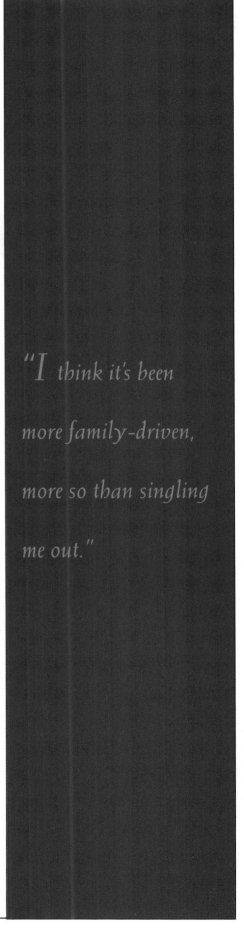

"*I think it's been more family-driven, more so than singling me out.*"

Home in the North Georgia Mountains

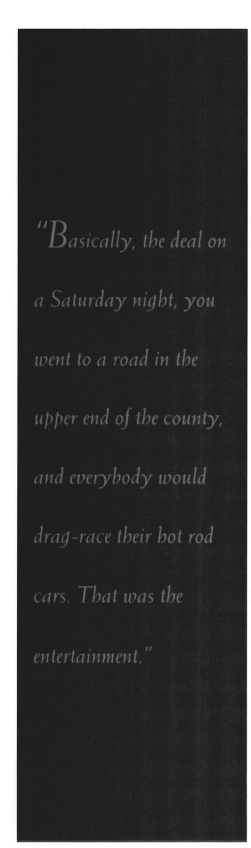

Forty years ago, Atlanta was a sedate but industrious city a world away from Dawson County, which lies forty miles from Peachtree Street and slightly east of due north. Atlanta at the time was just emerging as a business and transportation hub of the New South, and its sprawl across north and central Georgia had just begun.

As the century turns, Atlanta is pressing outward like a wave, with square miles of asphalt, huge new freeways spreading, and the new concrete, fresh paint, and bright sign lights of Hampton Inns and convenience markets aglow to the horizon at each new exit off Georgia 400 and Interstate 985, which spur up either side of the trendy Lake Lanier communities.

As the rush continues, the foothills town of Dawsonville will be just another exit number off the freeways.

"We're basically, for lack of a better term, a suburb of Atlanta," reckons Ernie Elliott, older brother of Bill. "Back then, at that point in time, you've got to understand that Atlanta was a long way off. You didn't go to Atlanta to have a good time. In the area we grew up in, there was nothing for recreation.

"We'd go to Atlanta once a month, maybe," Bill recalls. "That was a big deal. My mom would go down there to shop, down [U.S.] 19. There wasn't any freeway.

"We just didn't need to go there much. We always had a huge garden, over next to the store. It was big for that area, and we had pigs and cows. The first thing in the morning before school, me and Dan would take turns milking the cow. We grew vegetables and Mom canned them. She very seldom bought stuff."

No, Dawson and Lumpkin counties, home ground of the Elliotts and other north Georgia families, were pretty well self-contained, much as are other home grounds all along the Blue Ridge and Appalachian foothills, which run nearly the length of the East Coast.

The foothills are only fair for farming. Deep-cut by steep streams, the landscape brings isolation and encourages invention and self-reliance. If you don't do it yourself, it's not likely to get done. Folks are friendly, but they tend to their own business and don't waste time trying to mind yours.

North Georgia is gold country, site of one of America's first great gold rushes. It's also Cherokee country, ancient home of the tribe that inhabited much of the Southeast when settlers pushed into the mountains in the late 18th century.

Bill takes a minute to reflect. "Rowdy," Bill's Doberman pinscher, gets a loving pat on the head.

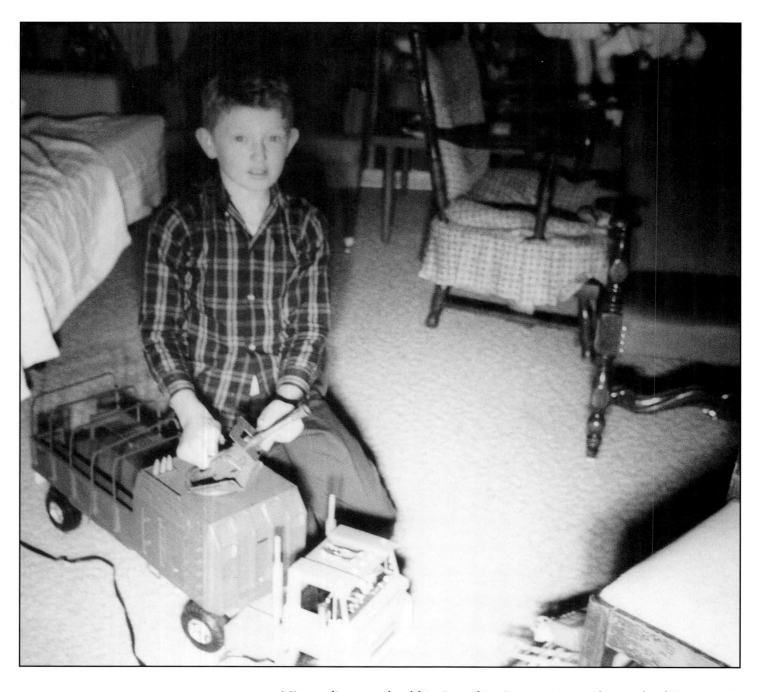

Above: The familiar comfort of home surrounds young Bill, who seems a bit surprised by the sudden photo op.

Right: George and Mildred's youngest of the couple's three sons, Bill, joined the family October 8, 1955.

Miners discovered gold in Lumpkin County, just to the north of Dawson, in 1828—part of a thin gold seam which outcrops in spots from Virginia through North Carolina into north Georgia. Along the Chestatee and Etowah rivers and by Yahoola Creek the metal turned up in such quantity that the United States government set up a coining mint at Dahlonega in 1838. That mint operated until the start of the Civil War. Today, the administration building of North Georgia College stands on the site of the old mint.

Gold mining, by various means (including a gigantic water cannon that blasted gold-bearing gravel out of the gullies and creekbeds), continued in the area into the 1920s and 1930s, and it's not unusual to find a few stray grains today. The big gold rush, however, was over by the 1850s.

Bill Elliott

Bill Elliott

Left: Best and brightest: George Elliott, 19 in 1943, served proudly in the United States Navy, one of a generation described as the finest our nation produced. George went on to produce a generation commendable in its own right.

Right and Below: Cindy and Bill are all smiles on their wedding day as they pose for the photographer.

Above: Mildred Elliott (left), mother of the three Elliott boys, visits with her mother, Audie Reece (right), beloved grandmother of the boys.

Left: Mrs. Elliott with Mary Catherine Cheuring.

Right: Bill learned to fly at a local airport in 1976, and holds ratings for Private Pilot, Single and Multi Engine Land, Instrument Airplane, Rotorcraft Helicopter, and CE-500. As with many top racers, from Cale Yarborough to Bobby Allison to Rusty Wallace, Bill finds solitude and relaxation in piloting a plane. These photos were taken by Bill's wife Cindy over the mountain ridge where the Blue Ridge Trail begins. This mountain ridge separates Dawsonville and Blairsville.

Bill Elliott

The gold rush, however, accelerated the rush of immigrants into the area, brought it prosperity, and made it settled. The government concluded a treaty with the Cherokee in order to move them farther west, then conducted a land lottery. A land rush thus followed the gold rush.

The Cherokee eventually were settled in Oklahoma. Oddly enough, when white settlement was permitted in Oklahoma Indian Territory in 1889, many of the western migrants came from north Georgia.

It isn't known what brought the Elliotts to north Georgia, although George Elliott and Mildred Reece—parents of Ernie, Dan, and Bill—could trace back a couple of generations. You have to imagine that both inherited the independence and self-reliance of their forebears and passed a good bit of that to their three sons.

George Elliott was a resourceful businessman, able to keep several concerns running at once. By the time his boys were on their feet, he had settled into a thriving building-supply business—Standard Supply Company—which operated out of a yard across the road from the Elliotts' home.

"Daddy was a lot like I am," says Ernie, whom you might describe as a very determined individual. "He wasn't real political, but I think everybody knew where he stood.

"He was pretty successful in most everything he did. He had a pretty unusual way of doing things, but that was Daddy. Regardless of how he did business, he was pretty successful at it, and he had a pretty large following of customers and clientele he dealt with.

"When he first had the [Ford] dealership, in '68 or '69, something like that, people who traded with him when that thing opened were still trading with him when he sold it [in the 1980s]."

Bill remembers it the same way. "You go around that area and talk to the older people, the only place they used to go to for building materials was Daddy's place," he says.

A little later, we'll get to the extraordinary lives of George and Mildred Elliott. For now, let's look around north Georgia and Atlanta, the big town which at the time was miles and miles away.

NASCAR racing, by the 1980s, had clustered in a small area of western North Carolina from Greensboro to Charlotte—"Charlotte" is the generic geography for the present homeland of NASCAR racing.

It's a shame that no one much recalls the sport's widespread origins. All along the Eastern foothills and in what is called the Piedmont, a red-clay zone stretching from Virginia to north Georgia, eager young fellows and hot Ford V8s mated to create a culture of easily available speed, a culture that spawned modern stock-car racing.

Right after World War II, there were several unofficial "hubs" of racing. In Virginia, racing sprung up around Norfolk and Richmond, and in the Southside, around Roanoke and Martinsville. In North Carolina, the game spread along the Piedmont axis from Greensboro and Asheboro, over to High Point, out to Wilkes County, then down through Alexander and Cabarrus counties to Charlotte.

Atlanta was the general hub in Georgia, with entrepreneurs such as Raymond Parks and Perry Smith and mechanics such as Red Vogt and Red Byron, NASCAR's first champion, came from Atlanta. The Flock brothers, NASCAR's first big stars, migrated to Atlanta and tied right in with racing. Jack Smith came from Sandy Springs.

Farther north, hotshots such as Lloyd Seay and Gober Sosebee, and racing businessmen such as Dahlonega's Frank Christian (perhaps one of the first to see opportunity in team ownership and sponsorship) grew out of gold country and established the early tone of a wild and growing sport. Frank's wife, Sarah, raced his cars for a while and made history by competing in NASCAR's first major event, at Charlotte in June 1949.

Much is made of the whiskey and moonshine aspect of early racing, and liquor was some part of the economy in north Georgia in the years before and after World War II. What many forget is that many of the men who "invented" racing after the war were warriors, boys who had been pulled out of sheltered areas such as north Georgia and southern Virginia and had been shoved headlong into Europe and the South Pacific.

Bill makes friends with the star attraction at SeaWorld, Shamu the Killer Whale

Running ahead of Dick May, Bill passes a full grandstand in his first Grand National race at North Carolina Motor Speedway in Rockingham, on February 29, 1976.

Right before the war, too, cars had become cheap (thanks in large part to Henry Ford's Models T and A), used cars and parts plentiful, and America's native mechanical ingenuity had gripped right on to cylinder heads and leaf springs. Hey, we can make these things go faster . . .

Now, bring a whole generation home from combat on the Rhine, landing planes on Okinawa, repairing Jeeps in motor pools around the world, hand them a little GI Bill money, and send them back home, where nothing was the same at all.

George Elliott, just home from Navy duty in the Pacific Ocean, was one of those.

"He was like a lot of other people," Ernie explains. "He'd served in the Pacific in World War II, and anybody who served in the military during that period of time—I don't think any of us who have never served in any kind of conflict like that really have any perception of what things were like. He'd come up during the Depression—that was another difficult time. I don't think any of us have any perception of what that was about.

Bill Elliott

"I think most boys are pretty much fascinated, or were at that time, with cars. They represented mobility that the Depression took away and the war pretty much deprived you of. So when Curtis Turner and all those guys raced around in those areas in the '40s and '50s, everybody was fascinated with that.

"I think Daddy was like everybody else. It was one of those deals—he enjoyed it, he wanted to do it. That took his mind off all the other stuff he had to deal with in the course of the day, so that's what he did."

George said more than once that organized racing was something he and his boys could do together, with the added benefit of keeping his three youngsters occupied, off the street, and out of trouble.

As racing matured from the twisty, two-lane roads of Dawson and Lumpkin counties, little dirt tracks sprung up all about. George Elliott and his oldest son Ernie, both natural tinkerers, merged opportunities and began hauling racing parts from track to track on weekends.

"Oh, we worked . . . there was a place called Cherokee Motor Speedway over there near Cartersville," Ernie remembers. "We worked Canton and Woodstock, which was called Dixie. They had a race track at Douglasville, we worked it. Rome. They had that one at Macon."

"Dixie's still there. I think they still run the race track at Douglasville. Rome's still there."

Certainly there is no racing without racers, and north Georgia was full of them, bred and grown out of the backroads and gullies where the gold had been. In the self-contained world of Dawson County, racing at Dixie and Douglasville was all anyone needed to know. No one cared to do more than race; no one cared to get better known.

"That's one of the things that has been a little disappointing over the years," Ernie notes. "For the amount of heritage that's there, the lack of [awareness] of what came out of there, and what it contributed to NASCAR, how little emphasis in the Atlanta media. It's almost like it's taken a back seat.

"Oh, who was from Macon? There was a lot of good racers from around in that area. I can think of a lot of guys who have just stayed there and raced locally—who could drive with anybody. Jody Ridley, Bud Lunsford, Doug Kenimer. All those guys. The Pryor boys from around Chattanooga. There was some pretty serious racing there in the early '60s."

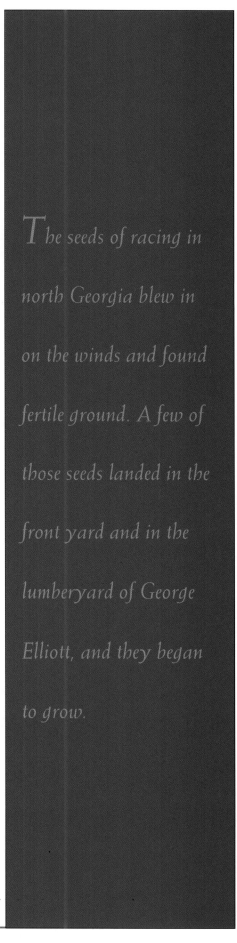

The seeds of racing in north Georgia blew in on the winds and found fertile ground. A few of those seeds landed in the front yard and in the lumberyard of George Elliott, and they began to grow.

Family

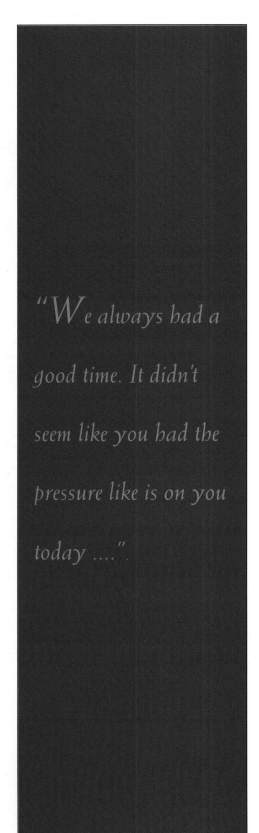

"We always had a good time. It didn't seem like you had the pressure like is on you today ...."

Geore Elliott was a remarkable man. Although plain and private in many aspects, his life story presents contradictions and paradoxes.

George, father of Ernie, Dan, and Bill, was a north Georgia native, born in 1924. Records show his birthplace as Lumpkin Campground, a settlement that grew from an old Methodist meeting ground in the eastern part of Dawson. The ground and structures are still in use, across the road from the Methodist church. In the well-tended churchyard are the graves of Elliotts, Reeces, Sosebees—the surnames of folks who worked land in the area for generations.

To the end of his life, George Elliott considered this spot home, calling it the most beautiful place on earth.

Like most young men of his time, he entered military service during World War II, leaving the hills to go to sea with the United States Navy. He saw duty at several American ports and in the South Pacific, thus getting a look at far more of the world than a north Georgia kid of that time could ever expect to see, and he spent several years in the Navy Reserve after the war, retiring from service with the rank of commander.

George's first order of business after the war, and on his return home, was to complete requirements for a bachelor of business administration degree from North Georgia College in Dahlonega. He also did post-graduate work on a master's degree in mathematics at Emory University in Atlanta, then took a job with Burroughs Machine Company in Fitzgerald, Georgia, far downstate. The Navy also required his reserve services at Brunswick, Georgia.

Before his discharge from active duty, George Elliott took part in a Navy program that enabled him to attend the University of Pennsylvania and Cornell University for studies in mathematics and physics. Once back home in Georgia, he was certified as a math teacher in 1953 and served a spell as principal at the Westside Elementary School in the county.

"He was very educated," oldest son Ernie says of his father, with pride.

George Elliott set up a building supply business at Dawsonville in the middle or late 1950s, and he did pretty well with it. He sold lumber, nails, structural steel, concrete block—whatever it took to erect a building in the area. George's business interests, and his growing family, kept him from completing his master's requirements.

Right: Chase and Brittany Elliott get a friendly hug from Disney World favorite "Minnie Mouse." Bill always makes time for his family, whether it be taking them along to the races or providing great hobbies . . . Starr Elliott pictured here on her horse.

In the late 1970s and early 1980s, George and family simultaneously ran the supply business and a Ford dealership up the road toward Dahlonega. That business developed into Bill Elliott Ford.

What kept George close to home was a young woman named Mildred Reece, who, records show, came from "Route 2, Dawsonville." Mildred, two years older than George, was in many ways as remarkable as her husband of 48 years. She completed high school at 14 and was valedictorian of her class.

Mildred, who completed a business course and followed with two years of college at North Georgia, showed an inclination to finer things. She came from a nice home (Mildred's mother, Audie "Mama" Reece, provided a foundation stone for the Elliott boys until her death in June 1991).

George and Mildred had been acquainted before he entered service, and on May 5, 1943, George Elliott and Mildred Reece became George and Mildred Elliott. The local paper notes that Mildred planned to travel to meet George after the marriage, as he was "in Baltimore, on defense work." She accompanied George through the remainder of his active service, and the couple returned home in 1946.

The union eventually produced three boys: Ernest George (Ernie), born August 25, 1947; Daniel Loy (Dan), born January 1, 1951; and William Clyde (Bill), who entered this world on October 8, 1955. All were born at Forsyth Hospital in the town of Cumming, one county back toward Atlanta. Bill was named for two cousins, William Elliott and Clyde Elliott.

Below: Elliott family Thanksgiving 1997.

All came home to the Elliotts' first home, a frame house there on postal Route 2, the road now named Elliott Family Parkway. That house is gone now, but there is great significance in the fact that the Elliotts' race shops, and Ernie's present engine and parts businesses, grew up adjacent to that site. In the late 1950s, the family took up residence in a brick house on the hill across the road.

Left: Chase and mom Cindy share a close bond, at home and at the race tracks.

Bottom Left: Older daughter Starr, child of Bill and first wife Martha, has grown to be a striking young woman.

Below: George Elliott and wife Mildred strike a pose at the NASCAR banquet.

Bottom Right: Brittany Elliott proves to be even more photogenic than her famous dad.

George and Mildred Elliott pose for a photo opportunity.

Bill Elliott

The Elliott family has always been extremely close and family is at the top of the list of Bill's priorities. *(Right)* From left to right Brittany, Trey Poole, Chase, and Kristin Poole. Trey and Kristin are Bill's niece and nephew. *(Below)* Ernie and his grandson Chris and Chase relax on the dock while daughter Nicki waits for a bite.

George Elliott has always been there to support his boys and help them to reach for the top.

George Elliott was a good businessman, a hard-working man, and though never wealthy, he was prosperous for his time and place. He had a keen eye for business ventures and was not afraid to take risks. He was successful, a man of means and influence in the county, but never ostentatious, and his manner and generosity made him scores of friends.

George also was very aware of the area's gold heritage and was an active numismatist, specializing in Dahlonega-minted coins. According to one story, he became interested in gold coins when a customer traded him a coin for a car. His collection developed to include many unique rarities, including three-dollar pieces, made only at Dahlonega.

George also invested in land, which offered additional return.

"We're not talking about the profit margins of today," Bill remembers. "With the property he had, if he had it today, he'd probably have a substantial fortune just from the land he'd acquired. But 10 or 12 years ago, land in Dawson County, you could get it for less than $1,000 an acre."

Bill Elliott

Yet, Bill also remembers a side of his father that combined frugal practicality with a touch of philanthropy. "Back then, the materials he couldn't sell, he'd go around the county and build rental houses, and I don't think he charged much rent."

From as far back as any of George's three sons can remember, their father played with race cars and racing, with oldest son Ernie taking the lead as parts-crafter and seller. George gained some influence in the stock-car circuits of north Georgia and eastern Tennessee. He attended what were then called Grand National races, at times towed his cars to them, and he got to know Bill France Sr., founder of NASCAR, and legendary figures such as Bobby Allison.

Yet, racing was a diversion for George; he had enough to do with his lumberyard, and later, his dealership. Bill remembers that "when Daddy bought the dealership, he left Mother to run the supply business, and she always was a part of that. Even when we were little, we'd do whatever you had to do, answer phones and all."

Ernie, who being the oldest got the first look at his father's racing efforts, remembers that George had his own ways of looking at the operation.

"The way Daddy raced," Ernie recalls with a laugh, "it was pretty funny. I'd see him go places and not even have a driver. Daddy would do the deal, he'd go to racetracks. You had to understand Daddy. The building supply business was a 24-hour-a-day job, and racing to him was his vacation.

"It was not a deal where he needed to go—he didn't have to go rent the car at the racetrack to somebody. He would just go and let somebody drive the car because he enjoyed racing, he legitimately enjoyed the sport. It was a source of income, but getting money off it was no big deal to him."

What really occupied George were his serious businesses, the lumberyard and later, the Ford dealership. Part of George's luck in making a family was in having three sons who could take over whatever they could handle, almost from the time they were born, much as farmers and small-town businessmen always have expected.

"We were slave labor," Bill says with a laugh. "Shoot, we never did nothing when we were young—Daddy kept us working, over there stacking two-by-fours or driving a forklift.

"That was just the way it was back then. Nowadays I guess it's child abuse. The thing of it is, things are so accessible now. There's too much media coverage of everything. Life gets too green on the other side, and the kids all venture out."

Not that there were not opportunities for the Elliott boys. All, of course, graduated from high school. Ernie and Dan followed their parents through the curriculum at North Georgia College and came out with degrees. Bill wasn't quite so sure he wanted to go down that road.

"By the time they got to me, I told them not to waste their money," Bill says with a smile.

Ernie backs that up. "Education is not a prerequisite for success," he explains. "School's for some people, and other people it's not for.

"My oldest daughter, she graduated from North Georgia. My youngest daughter, she lasted a week. She absolutely hates school, and there was no need making her go. When it's that way, if things are going to be that miserable, there's no need doing it."

George and Mildred were strict parents and did not spare the rod, "or the stick, or the two-by-two, or whatever he could find," Bill recalls. "But you know, he was military, and discipline was just the way it was as he understood it."

He recalls a few colorful stories, reaching back to summer days as he grew to his early teens.

"There was a pile of gravel back there behind the supply house," Bill remembers, again with a laugh. "One day I was just back there throwing rocks out into the woods. Daddy had a bunch of old windows he'd picked up somewhere, and he'd stacked them up out there. Man, when he saw me throwing those rocks, he really showed me 'what-fer'."

The Elliotts had ties to the Methodist Church. Bill, the youngest, somehow sidestepped church-going as a youngster, "but we were taught right from wrong," he says righteously.

With a full NASCAR schedule to contend with, Bill rarely gets time away from the track. On the rare occasions he can, he enjoys skiing with friends or a relaxing ride in a glider plane as seen here. (Left) Bill with long-time friend Harry Melling. (Below) Bill enjoys a day on the slopes with Curtis Colwell and Lamar Paris.

Bill Elliott

What all the Elliott boys remember most is work, plain hard work.

"When that building supply started, I don't think anybody realized how much business and how much work there was involved in that deal," Ernie says.

"I remember in '57—the only reason I remember the date is that Daddy bought the first brand-new truck he ever bought in '57—I can remember riding with him. He'd work at the building supply during the day, and at night he'd drive that thing to Birmingham, Alabama, to pick up steel, then drive back that night, then work all day the next day. That's work.

"We went to school, went to college, and worked in the lumber yard, same as Dan."

Bill also recalls running long-haul errands for his father as a teenager (with clues that he may have been behind the wheel before he had his Georgia driver's license). When all hands were busy elsewhere, Bill was elected to drive the tractor rig.

"I'd haul material as far out as Copperhill, Tennessee, and all over north Georgia," he recalls.

What he recalls more is plain, hard, physical work. Bill went right into action when his father built the block building for the supply business around 1960, give or take a year.

"I can remember them hauling dirt in there with a dump truck, and I'd have to pack it," he says. "I had one of these hand deals, a tamping deal. All it was was like a six-by-twelve piece of wood with a long board and two handles nailed on it, and you'd stand up and pound the dirt in.

"We just did whatever it took. We worked on that building for a lot of years. It was like an aftermarket project."

Regular work and racing began to grow side-by-side in the late 1960s. Ernie, having tried his hand at street racing, was drawn into it as George's racing parts business took hold.

"I built motors and stuff, fooled with race cars," Ernie recalls. "You know, when you were kind of like I was, which was sort of like he was, he'd drag me off to these race tracks.

"I couldn't tell you I was real interested in it in the first place. But if they take you every weekend, you either start to love it or despise it. So that was kind of the deal. It's not only a way to make a living, but something you enjoyed."

Bill, eight years Ernie's junior, never hot-rodded. By the time Bill came along, law enforcement in Dawson County had become a good bit more sophisticated.

"Used to be you'd try to outrun the sheriff, but it was you against him, and it was almost kind of a game," Bill says. "Later on, it was you against everybody with radios."

But, as with everything the Elliotts did, there was more than enough work to go around, and Bill, like Ernie and Dan, was caught up in it.

"The best I remember, we had an old parts truck in the late '60s—Daddy was still in the building-materials business. Daddy would go to all the races Friday night, Saturday night, even Sunday night, and sell parts. It was just a cab-over truck with a van body, and we pulled a trailer.

"I'm sure I either drove the truck or I was in a car following the truck. I've done it all, from sweeping the floor, to painting the car, to bondoing it to putting engine pieces together.

"When Ernie had the speed shop there, I used to go in—I'd do everything from grinding cylinder heads, helping him build motors, to working on street cars, putting on headers and stuff on street cars. I'd do the aluminum work, sheet-metal work, on and on and on."

All work and no play? Not exactly. Work was play, at least on the racing side. And Bill has pleasant memories of a close-knit family in a small town.

"I guess the biggest thing I miss about the time we were growing up was we always got together at the holidays, whether it be Thanksgiving or Christmas," Bill remembers. "We always had big family deals with lots of food, and it was a big thing, with all the family there. That's the biggest thing I miss today.

"We always had a good time. It didn't seem like you had the pressure like is on you today—you've got to be here, got to be there. Everybody just came in and enjoyed that special moment at Thanksgiving and Christmas. Everything's hustle and bustle now.

"Even when you're trying to relax, there's too much to do now. I've got to take my boat to the lake, got to go fishing, got to go skiing, do this, do that. You don't have time to enjoy the values. Back then, we had nothing else to do—there was nothing else to do. We didn't have a ballgame in town, or a drive-in, or a show."

What they did have was racing, which became the center of gravity as the boys grew up.

"I guess the biggest thing that drove us was that Daddy was so involved in it," Bill says. "He always went to races, he always had some sort of race cars, somehow, some way. We got involved in selling parts, then started doing motors for dirt-track cars around there—this, that, and the other. I was so into cars, that just kind of led me into working on the race cars."

The first "race" car Bill considered his own was "a '57 Ford," he says. "We always had Fords. It was wore out when I got it, just an old two-door coupe.

"Seems like Ernie had it. Ernie traded around and got it somewhere, and he sold it to me for like $25 or $40—that was big money to me back then. It seems like I had to work it out because I worked for Ernie then.

"It was a road car, but I was going to make a race car out of it. I got it all stripped out, cut the top off it, and I was trying to put a roll cage in it and all that stuff. Daddy realized I was pretty serious, so he said, 'Well, maybe we ought to just go out and buy you something."

Next up was "a '63 Fairlane somebody had used as a race car. I drove it a little bit. That was about when [Jody] Ridley was driving a Falcon, so Daddy bought a Falcon from some guy who had run it two or three times and run out of money. He bought it and a motor and the whole bit. I think Daddy gave about $2,200 for it—that was a lot of money back then.

"It had new motor parts—the motor was tore all apart—a new quick-change rear end in it, just a lot of good stuff. Then Ernie and I went in there and rebuilt the thing and started back racing. We were pretty successful with that car."

George sensed his sons' enthusiasm and aptitude for racing, and he quietly encouraged them in races and tryouts at Dixie Speedway and other area tracks. Ernie gave it a run for a while, and so did Dan, but both had other projects that took time and focus.

Dan was in college at North Georgia. Ernie was building race cars and already was enlisting local drivers to run them. Bill, who had picked up

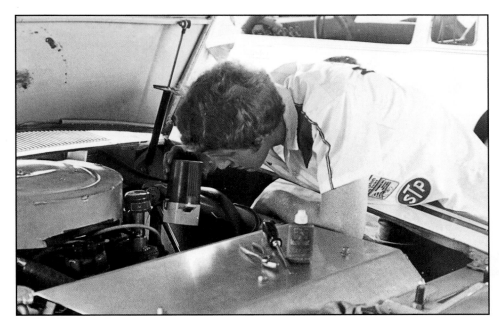

the race-car craft quickly at his brother's shop, came to the track with a fresh, clear view.

"We were watching him practice, and I said to Daddy, 'There's your driver'," Ernie says. "That was pretty plain to see. I'd tried driving, but I wasn't talented enough to drive—not any kind of driver, really.

"He was really . . . ," Ernie begins, looking for the right word. "I think a driver has to be pretty focused on what they're doing. You can't be thinking about, 'Well, if I change this or change that, am I going to make the deal better or worse.' I think they pretty much have to drive it and just tell you what the car needs. It was pretty clear he was just really good at that."

Actually, Bill remembers it the other way around. He says he enjoyed working on the cars more than driving them, and that the racing and driving, to him, helped validate the work he'd done on the car, the changes he'd made.

Not that working on the cars was without perils.

"Back then we had stock frames and stock bodies," Bill explains. "I've cut up many '56 Fords and '65 Falcons with a torch in my day. The Falcon was a uni-body. The Ford had rails and the Falcon didn't, so you'd cut the rails out from under a '56 Ford and shorten them, then put the roll cage on it, then cut the body off the unibody of the '65 Falcon.

"I spent more of my time going to the junkyard, because every time you wrecked, you went to a junkyard and looked for a '56 Ford to get the control arms off it. That's true. That's just the way it was.

"The hardest thing to do when you were cutting the body off a car back then was they used a lot of undercoating material inside the car. You'd catch it on fire [with the torch] and it would burn it up—plus the briar patch and every-thing else. You never cut one up inside."

Bill and Ernie began racing for real at Dixie in 1974, and Bill quickly began gathering up trophies. He won a lot of races that first year, and he and the little band of family and volunteers ventured out some, to Cleveland, Tennessee, and Macon, Georgia.

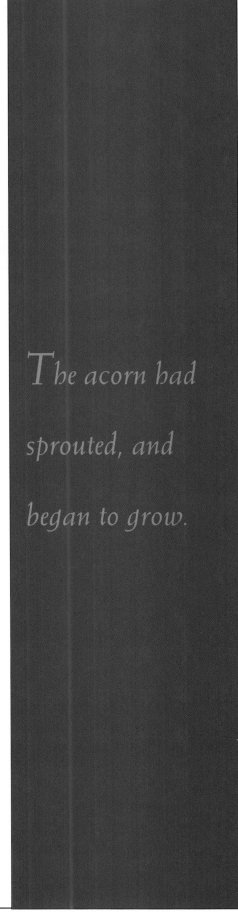

The acorn had sprouted, and began to grow.

The Elliotts Go Racing

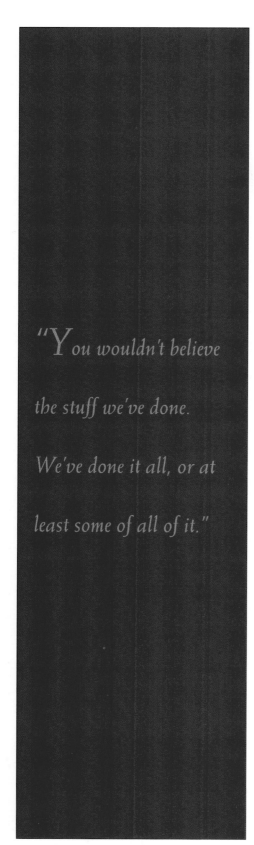

"*You wouldn't believe*

the stuff we've done.

We've done it all, or at

least some of all of it."

Two words, *family* and *work*, pointed the Elliott clan, and Bill in particular, toward the destiny that chose them. There were few distractions in the rural hills around tiny Dawsonville, and the hard-working Elliotts stayed plenty busy within their own domain, which centered on George's businesses and his hobbies—cars and racing.

As Bill grew through his teens, his life and times entwined with the family's fortunes, as if by nature. George and Mildred's various endeavors required full-time attention and involved their three boys from sunup to past dark.

"He made a living," Bill says simply of his father. "He worked and made a living. When he got the Ford dealership and couldn't get anybody to look after it,

It's clear that Bill's interest in cars started at an early age. Many years have passed and Bill still can't live without them. It has been a pleasant career choice, as can be seen at right.

George Elliott was a successful businessman running a home supply business, an auto salvage business, and a Ford dealership.

Bill Elliott

he went and ran it, and Mother ran the building supply business and I drove the truck for her. I worked at the building supply business with Dan, then he worked at the car dealership up to '72.

"They worked hard. They really, really worked hard. They worked from early in the morning to late at night all the time, and we were expected to do whatever it took to help, whether it be answering the phone, helping customers who came in wanting material, or driving the truck.

"You wouldn't believe the stuff we've done. We've done it all, or at least some of all of it. We didn't go on very many vacations. For us, fun was going to races on Friday, Saturday, Sunday. We never played any stick-and-ball. They wouldn't let us compete in any school sports because we had to work. We were expected to be at the building supply. Even when I was real little, I answered the phone.

"I was driving the [delivery] truck when I was 12, 13, 14, I'm dead serious. I drove to Dallas, Georgia, when I was 13, driving a tractor-trailer. We did everything, I'm telling you. Sheila [Ernie's wife] used to go with me when I had my learner's license."

The Elliott family patriarch, George (pictured at left), managed to run the family businesses and yet still found time to participate in the family hobby, which later became the family's biggest venture. When possible, he also made it to the races and was on hand to share in the victory celebration (above) with his sons, from left to right, Dan, Bill, and Ernie.

Ernie had shown aptitude with the small-block V8s folks raced in north Georgia at the time. With a nudge from his father, Ernie acquired equipment to run a speed shop, an outgrowth of George's weekend racing-parts business. Bill, of course, veered in that direction. It was all part of the job, the family job.

"I was a senior in high school," Bill recalls. "I started working for him at the speed shop. I was making $100 a week—heck, that was big money."

Meanwhile, as noted, Bill had become the driver of the family. Ernie had street-raced some but wasn't interested in turning circles. Dan, quick and smart, looked like the man for a while.

"I got Dan into it," George Elliott said once, "and I thought he was going to be the one because he was quick as a cat in everything he did, but he didn't like it either. Bill was the one."

At the very start, Bill's racing was simply the next thing to do, the next chore of the family's checklist. In addition to parts, George fielded race cars at area tracks—Dixie, Jeffco, Chattanooga, and so on. As his interest grew, so did his circle of acquaintances, which came to include NASCAR founder Big Bill France and Bill Gazaway, Georgia neighbor and NASCAR's competition director. Before long, George had branched far out and was taking sportsman-type cars to big races at Daytona, Charlotte, and Rockingham.

George thus glimpsed the big picture and came to see opportunity. George Elliott was one of many who came to share France's vision of a sport with a spectacular future, and in his stubbornly individual way, he contributed to it.

Long before it became stressful, racing was fun for Bill. Only when the demands from sponsors and fans and the expectation of winning became almost consuming did Bill's intensity (right) become obvious. But he handles it quite well and still manages to keep his smile and warm, friendly demeanor. That's why his fans consistently select him as "Most Popular Driver."

"Daddy, he was involved in the racing deal," Bill says. "He knew those guys real well, and he owned part of some of the racetracks. He was in with some partners who ran Jeffco Speedway. I did everything from taking tickets to selling stuff at the concession stands."

The strategy, if not the tactics, trickled down to his sons, with Bill gradually anointed as driver. Bill reaches way back to find the roots of his racing. He remembers horsing around with hot rods as a teenager with cousin Tim Byrd and neighborhood pal Rooster Ingram.

"I remember, my cousin, we were about the same age and went to school together, we'd slip off after the race [wherever] was over, to the dealership," Bill remembers. "Daddy had two Shelby Mustangs, and me and [Tim] would slip out the back gate and go over there and turn circles."

Moonshine tripping had all but vanished by the time the Elliott boys were coming up, so don't be tempted to connect the Elliotts with the old liquor trade, in any way. But the car-crazy legacy, with road racing and "clowning" (local vernacular for cutting up in cars) remained. George Elliott, in the manner of fathers everywhere, was determined to herd his boys out of harm's way.

"Actually, I got my boys into racing because I wanted them to stay away from the back roads," George said once. "If they were going to be driving fast, I wanted them to do it in the right place."

With the boys fully occupied in the family's work corral, the move to the next square was almost inevitable. George arranged with the promoter at Macon, Georgia, to let 16-year-old Bill enter a support-class race in April 1972. Driving a primered Ford Mustang, Bill drove impressively, finishing third or so—no one really remembers.

Exactly *why* Bill started racing mystifies even Bill. It was the next thing to do, the natural way to go, that's all.

"I don't know if anybody's asked me why I started," Bill wonders. "I was just so exposed to all that stuff. When I was helping Ernie sell parts at the racetracks, we went Friday night, Saturday night, Sunday afternoon, Sunday night. I was exposed to so much racing.

"It just seemed like I didn't know if it was really what I wanted to do, but I thought, 'Well, I'd like to try it a little bit.' I always worked hard on the cars. Ernie drove and Dan drove, but Ernie didn't care much for it. Dan, he drove some, but he was going to college and stuff.

"I guess the biggest thing that drove us was that Daddy was so involved in it. He always had some sort of race cars, somehow, some way. I was always so into cars, and that kind of led me into working on the race cars.

"I was just able to pursue it. I don't know that I really thought anything, other than just about working on the cars. I promise you, I felt more comfortable working on it. Working on it was the first priority, driving it was second. I enjoyed working on them so much that driving was secondary, seeing if what you did made it better."

In 1973, Bill began racing regularly at Dixie Speedway in Woodstock, Georgia, which pretty much became his home track. Among the regulars at Dixie (and elsewhere) was local legend Jody Ridley, who became young Bill's early hero.

"We ventured out a little bit [from Dixie]," Bill says. "We ran Macon, some up in Chattanooga, ran some dirt, ran Jefferson. That was about it. I kind of bounced around there, doing a little bit of racing. I was helping Jody and them, and Ernie was helping them with their motor stuff."

Bill waved the checkered flag out of his window celebrating his first victory of his career in early 1974 at the Dixie Speedway.

photo by Dozier Mobley.

The first car Bill really got familiar with was "a '57 Ford, just a two-door coupe," Bill recalls. "We've always had Fords. It was wore out when I got it. It seems like Ernie had it, traded around and got it somewhere, sold it to me for like $25 or $40. That was big money back then. Seems like I had to work it out.

"That was a road car, not a race car. I was going to make a race car out of it. I went over there and got it all stripped out, cut the top off of it, trying to put a roll cage in it and all that stuff. Daddy realized I was pretty serious, and he said, 'Maybe we ought to just go out and buy you something.' It laid over there in the junkyard forever and a day.

"Then we had a '63 Fairlane somebody had used as a race car. I drove it just a little bit. Daddy had some other guys build it. That's when Ridley was driving a Falcon. We bought a Falcon from this guy who had run two or three races then run out of money, bought it and the motor and the whole bit. I think Daddy gave like $2,200 for it.

It had new motor parts, the motor was torn apart, a new quick-change rear end in it, just a lot of good stuff. Ernie and I went in there and rebuilt the thing and started back racing. We were pretty successful with that car."

After Bill's first win at Dixie Motor Speedway, he began to accumulate a rack of undated Dixie trophies and Jeffco at Commerce but mainly Dixie trophies and a reputation as a cool, clean competitor who seldom bent the equipment—and as a winner.

Like Prospero in *The Tempest*, George continued to urge his sons in the direction of his vision. His 19-year-old had taken root as a racer and had shown talent. Bill was content where he was, focused entirely on the north Georgia world of race cars and little tracks. George saw more.

"I was content to run Dixie Speedway every Saturday night," Bill says. "He was like, 'Maybe we should go to this.' He had some cars he bought, that one old Torino he bought from Junie Donlavey. Junie had bought it from Holman-Moody or somebody. Daddy'd say, 'Well, let's take that thing to Charlotte and try to run the sportsman race,' something like that. What am I going to do, tell him no?"

George and Bill tried twice, in the preliminaries at Charlotte in 1974 and 1975. Both times the car came up short in qualifying. Not at all discouraged, George decided his son needed a real race car, a Grand National car.

In the mid-1970s, racing was different. No one looked at Winston Cup as a big-budget impossible dream. A youngster with a little backing and the right motivation could catch the tail end of the field.

Look at the race rosters in those days. Sure, you had the big dogs like Richard Petty, David Pearson, Cale Yarborough, Buddy Baker, the Allison brothers, Benny Parsons, and even a headstrong outsider named Darrell Waltrip. Then came a group of mid-liners: Richard Childress, Cecil Gordon, Dick Brooks, Coo Coo Marlin, Elmo Langley, and Walter Ballard.

Everything else was wide open, and if a kid was ready and fast, he had as much a chance as anyone to (a) qualify, (b) run 15th or 20th, and maybe even (c) surprise the crowd with a second, fourth, or sixth. This environment bred a generation of newcomers, including Dale Earnhardt, Ricky Rudd, Terry Labonte—and Bill Elliott. The year was 1976.

Bill remembers the beginning with a laugh. George came across a Ford Torino, updated to 1975 bodywork. The car was a good bit older, had been wrecked, and came with a peculiar pedigree.

"That thing was a piece of junk," Bill says now. "The inspectors wouldn't even come around it, afraid they'd get ptomaine poisoning. I know you had to have your tetanus shot to work on it.

"It was a Torino. Richie Panch drove it his rookie year in '72, and it had been wrecked a bunch of times. My dad traded Bobby Allison out of it; I think Bobby had picked it up in some kind of settlement, doing whatever he was doing, building cars back then. It had some questionable history, and it was a tank—3,800 pounds with no lead."

The star in the sights was the 1-mile track at Rockingham, North Carolina, then known as North Carolina Motor Speedway. The 500-mile race at the Rockingham track, in 1976, was the fourth on the season calendar, behind Riverside, Daytona, and Richmond.

"My dad pushed me in that direction," Bill recalls. "I didn't feel like I was ready to go. He wanted me to go run Rockingham and Atlanta and all these places, and I was very reluctant to go.

"It was something I look back on and I think he might have seen more in me than I saw in myself. He was saying, 'You need to go do this,' although he didn't come right out and say it. It was just one of those deals that was kind of matter-of-fact, 'We need to do this and need to do that.'

Very early in his career, Bill ran strong at Darlington. In 1977's Southern 500, running with number 52 on his car, Bill finished a strong 10th place. It was only a preview of things to come. Within 10 years, Darlington would give Bill his most famous title: "Million Dollar Bill"!!

Few fans know that Bill drove an Oldsmobile in one race at Atlanta in November 1978.

Bill Elliott

"His involvement in racing through the years—he knew France Sr. and all that deal, how NASCAR got started and all the people that were involved—he realized this sport was going to be the one that made it to the next step."

George and his sons, plus a group of cousins and neighbors, loaded up and hauled the Ptomaine Torino 250 miles to Rockingham. "It was just people who could get off work and go hang out with us," Bill recollects. "We didn't pay anybody. We had 12 or 15 people, and it was a pretty motley-looking crew.

"It was unbelievable. We'd take the mattress and the box spring—somebody got the mattress and somebody the box spring, and some of us slept in the truck and some in the car."

Bill got the car in the race, the Carolina 500, qualifying 34th. He made only 32 of the 492 laps, falling out with a broken oil pump, and finished 33rd. Richard Petty won by two laps, leaving Bill Elliott's debut somewhere below a footnote. The family's take for the weekend's work was $640.

George Elliott, however, saw farther than one try and one check. Mostly on his own dime, he entered Bill in six other races that season—Talladega, Atlanta, summer Daytona, Michigan, Pocono, and Nashville. His best finish was 14th at Nashville, in a Ford owned by Bill Champion. For the summer's work, the Elliotts counted up $11,635, hardly enough to cover expenses.

Almost from the start, Bill's cars carried number 9. During his short-track association with the Ridleys, he occasionally ran number 97, number 98, and number 9. When time came to choose a number for their early entries, the Elliotts settled on number 9.

It's almost impossible, in racing terms, to think of Bill Elliott without number 9, or vice versa. Like Richard Petty with number 43 or Dale Earnhardt with number 3, you don't think of one without thinking of the other.

Despite George Elliott's racing connections and sound business sense, he and his raw troupe remained in many ways green as Georgia grass. Most of the time, the boys were buried to their eyeballs in preparing the cars and engines and had little time to look around at the wide world.

In addition, the isolation of a mountain town creates a small world, limited to home and a few outlying towns—Dahlonega, Cleveland, Gainesville. Certainly the Elliott boys had seen something of the outside, in materials trips to Birmingham and Atlanta and in racing trips to Chattanooga and Macon. But those travels always ended at home, at Standard Supply or at the speed shop, with the tunnel vision of heads-down work all the way.

That's pretty much the way the Elliott's approached their early tries at the big-time. These were racing trips, much like the ones to Macon or Dixie or Jeffco, except longer, farther, more expensive. Bill, his father, and his brothers put their shoulders to the load much as they always had at home: work on the car, make it fast, go race.

There is a sweet naiveté to the family's early efforts, as they persisted on faith and a few dollars. As with many successful start-ups, the Elliott's flew blindly, with no idea they were supposed to fail. A more recent case, and maybe the last of its kind, was that of the late Alan Kulwicki, 1992 Winston Cup champion, who came south from Wisconsin in the mid-1980s and, as he put it, "just blindly went forward and figured it out later."

In order to be competitive, the old Torino gave way to a sleek red Mercury. It brought Bill another top ten in his first Daytona 500.

Bill was not only running with some of NASCAR's biggest stars, he was also finishing ahead of them. It would still be some time before the right people would notice.

"I think I'm still naïve to it," Bill says frankly. "I do it not to be in Winston Cup, I do it because I enjoy driving. That's the key to anything, whether it's here or driving a go-cart on Saturday night or a hobby dirt car, to me it would be no different. I never came into this sport saying this is what it will be and that's it. I just came into it doing the best job I could, and wherever it fell, it fell, and that was it.

"When I started, it was like, well, we had to run good enough to make races. Then when we made races we had to run good enough to finish races. Then it was middle of the pack, back of the pack, middle of the pack, now you're starting to get toward the front of the pack. Everything was a stepping stone."

Even with the Elliotts' native abilities and blind desire, the hurdle was equipment. Bill never was comfortable in the rough Torino. Driving for others was chancy and, really, never was an option in the Elliott playbook. Early in the 1977 season, George scouted around for a new car.

It just happened that car owner Roger Penske (in one of his short-lived early forays into stock cars) and driver Bobby Allison had reached the end of the road, and Penske, fully occupied with champ cars and Formula One. With Allison as broker, George acquired a turnkey 1977 Mercury, a major step up for the Elliott family team.

Bill ran 10 races in 1977, beginning at Rockingham in March, where he finished 30th in the old Torino, with a broken clutch. He was 32nd at Atlanta (broken engine), 15th in Charlotte's World 600 (15 laps down), 15th at Michigan (eight laps down), and 35th in his first-ever run at Daytona, falling out after 46 laps with the steam gauge pegged.

Bill Elliott

Elliott's first race with the Mercury, at Talladega in August, was encouraging. Starting 20th, he ran at the leaders' pace until a brake problem cut his day short just past halfway. The car, and Bill, showed better at Charlotte in October, where he ran all the way and finished 10th, and at Atlanta in November, where again he took the finish flag, recording 11th place in a rain-shortened event.

NASCAR's annual record book took note the next January, including him for the first time. Bill Elliott, Dawsonville, Georgia, is listed at a skinny 6'1", 150 pounds, with the notation: "Bill Elliott increased his Winston Cup activity in 1977 and improved his performance statistics a great deal. He notched two tenth-place finishes—one at Darlington and another at Charlotte. He started short-track racing in 1974 and moved up to Winston Cup competition in 1976. The youngster bears watching—with the right equipment, he could be a strong contender."

That began to prove true in 1978, when Bill, running another carefully budgeted 10-race schedule, began to open some eyes. Again driving the Mercury, Elliott gridded eighth and finished ninth, five laps down, in his first-ever Daytona 500. He backed that up with ninth at Darlington (the tough old track where Bill, from the start, did well), an impressive sixth at Talladega, another ninth at Daytona's summer Firecracker, and a sixth in the Southern 500.

With no outside money to speak of (the car was listed most of the year as the *Dahlonega Ford Sales Ford*, after George's dealership), Elliott had made top 10 in five of his 10 starts for a 15.7 finish average and $42,065 in purse. George said later he'd figured about $10,000 per race (a fraction of what the good teams spent), so the rewards came nowhere close to reimbursement.

One little secret, hidden away by time: In Atlanta's Dixie 500, Bill's last race of the season, Bill drove an Oldsmobile—that's right, an *Oldsmobile*—marking one of the very few times in his life he raced anything but a Ford.

"Daddy borrowed it from L.G. DeWitt back when Benny [Parsons] was driving for him in the late '70s," Elliott admits. "Back then, they had the real boxy cars, and Oldsmobile had the best one, when Junior and Cale won so many races in the Oldsmobile. We just wanted to try it in one race." Bill ran fairly well but dropped out after 80 laps with a broken valve.

As Bill notes, "everything was a stepping stone" in those days, and most of those steps led upward, although progress was not steady. The family again penciled in 10 races in the Mercury, beginning at Atlanta in March, where Elliott got caught in an early wreck and had to quit after 61 laps. Amazingly, that was the first time the Mercury got bent, nearly two years after George acquired it from Bobby Allison. The next time out, a month later, Elliott drove the repaired Cat to seventh at Darlington, and he followed with a sixth at Talladega.

From mid-year on came a series of small breakthroughs. The Elliott's ran their first-ever race at Michigan in June, with help from Jim and Jan Knutson, local RV and snowmobile dealers. The Knutsons, who remain close with the Elliotts today, later played a role in a big career break for the team. More to follow . . .

The real shocker came at the Southern 500 at Darlington in September. Bill qualified a career-best sixth and brought it home second, two laps behind childhood idol David Pearson, meanwhile leading the first few laps of his Winston Cup career, staying on the track while the leaders pitted during caution on lap 116 and again on lap 162.

Running in Atlanta's Dixie 500 in November 1977, Bill passes Donnie Allison.

At that same race, Ernie gained some notice as Sears/Craftsman's top crew chief, joining the likes of Maurice Petty, Leonard Wood, and Buddy Parrott among 1979's award winners. There really was not a hierarchy among the Elliott team. At that time NASCAR required that a team designate a crew chief, and Ernie was it, almost by default.

That Southern 500 really was an icebreaker for a couple of reasons. First, it showed that the changing of the guard, from the 1930s generation to the 1950s one, was right over the hill. Behind Bill on the final chart came rookie Terry Labonte (third) and newcomer Ricky Rudd (eighth). Another young hot rod, Dale Earnhardt (who was not at Darlington), went on to win rookie of the year.

Second, George's lifelong devotion to Ford caught the eye of the make's fervent fans. There were only eight Ford products in the 40-car field, including the Junie Donlavey Mercury of Rudd and the Bud Moore Thunderbird of Bobby Allison. El-liott was the only Ford intruder among an all-Chevrolet top seven.

Here, another confession: Roger Hamby, injured in a wreck at Pocono in July, had a sponsorship commitment from Kings Inn and needed a driver to help him fill the card. Elliott drove the Hamby Chevrolet—*Chevrolet*—at three races down the stretch, finishing 10th at Bristol, 11th at Richmond (his first two short-track starts), and 23rd at Rockingham. In return, Kings Inn, a motel chain, joined up with the Elliotts' Mercury at Darlington, where he ran Hamby's number 17.

In all, Elliott drove 13 races in 1979, officially earning $57,330 and inching his finish average forward to 14.3. With 1980 upcoming, the NASCAR record book offered this entry: "Bill Elliott pulled a surprise attack on the NASCAR Winston Cup racing community when he climbed into the cockpit of the No. 17 Mercury at the 1979 Southern 500 and wheeled his way to a second-place finish behind winner David Pearson. At the same time, his brother Ernie took top honors that day in the Sears/Craftsman Pit Crew Competition. Bill competes in several races each season and impressed everyone with his driving ability, but has never been able to put together a full-fledged campaign on the Winston Cup trail."

The problem, as George had come to know, was simple economics. Purse money didn't pay the freight, and the more races the fledgling group ran, the more a season cost. Bill had begun to pick up bit-at-a-time sponsorships, no more than a couple hundred dollars at a time. The little family combo had reached a hump, and by themselves they could not get over it.

Country-proud and independent—and too busy *racing*, besides—the Elliotts seldom sought help. What help there was came from the few regulars who admired the Elliott's' heads-down, determined style, including legendary car owner Bud Moore (who cross-pollinated with Ernie on engine tuning) and his driver, Benny Parsons. George, meanwhile, scoured his network of racing connections and pieced together little week-to-week money deals.

George had put all he had into the dream—his dream, his sons' dream. There are wild estimates, none confirmed by book, that George spent close to $1 million from the late 1960s to 1980 to help his boys along.

"I didn't have that kind of money," George told a writer some time later. "Each time we raced, I was down $10,000. Bobby Allison was spending $70,000 a race, and I could only dream of $70,000. To make it in racing, especially in a small operation, you've got to watch your pennies and budget your time."

Performance wasn't the problem; Bill and Ernie's strong show at Darlington the previous September had shown that. At the start of 1980, George Elliott determined to get his gang on the superhighway or go home.

With spare change from the Knutsons, Bill finished 12th in the 1980 Daytona 500, but a troubling slide followed—29th at Atlanta (engine), 21st at Talladega (last car running), dead last at Charlotte (wreck on lap 7). He steadied the ship with a ninth in June at Michigan, his newfound home away from home, adding a 12th in the Firecracker, a seventh at Tal-ladega, and another ninth at Michigan. Then, at Darlington, normally his demonstration track, he limped home 33rd with a broken oil pump. The check that weekend came to $1,625, for all it mattered.

NASCAR then turned up the wick in September, announcing that in 1981 all cars would run on a 110-inch wheelbase, down from the old 115-inch standard. To George Elliott, that meant a new car, and there was nothing close to that in the budget. The clock was ticking toward sundown.

Bill Elliott

Sidelined by injury, Roger Hamby hired Bill to drive his Chevrolet number 17 for several races in 1979.

☐ Yes, we are interested in helping support the "JACKSON SPECIAL" and have checked below the amount of our participation. Our check is enclosed.

		FULL HELP	PART HELP	LITTLE HELP
June 15	Michigan	$100.00	$ 50.00	$ 25.00
July 4	Daytona	100.00	50.00	25.00
Aug. 17	Michigan	100.00	50.00	25.00
Total Amount Enclosed		☐ $300.00	☐ 150.00	☐ 75.00

Without a top sponsor to pick up the expenses, the Elliott team was still struggling to pay its way. Race to race, bills were paid with various sponsors on the car. Focused on their goal, the Elliott family held on through those early years.

A local decal painter pictured here scribing sponsors' names on the car.

Bill Elliott

The rest of this story is pretty well known, and it's become a heartening fable for others who have come to the brink. In it, all at once, come the Elliotts' honest determination, recognition of it by their peers, and an assist at each base by a few good friends.

It all came down to the NAPA National 500 at Charlotte in October. George had decided to make that race, one way or another. Charlotte promoter H.A. "Humpy" Wheeler, had arranged a promotion with the Buck Stove company, under which a winner and a non-winner would be paired, with their average finishes to be compared against those of other pairs for a grand prize. Non-winner Bill, with averages in the low to mid teens, paired up with old friend Benny Parsons.

Parsons was driving M.C. Anderson's number 27 Chevrolet, with sponsorship from Melling Tool Company of Jackson, Michigan. Harry Melling's firm manufactured SAE oil pumps, gears, and other automotive and industrial parts. Melling, at the time, was launching a line of engine-timing components called Mell-Gear. At Parsons's urging, Melling agreed to offer the Elliotts $500 for the Charlotte race.

The Elliotts showed up with Mell-Gear lettered on the quarter-panels.

Parsons had a flat tire and wrecked, finishing 33rd. Bill had one of his top runs of the season, racing home sixth, just two laps behind winner Dale Earnhardt. (By the way, Ricky Rudd, Kyle Petty, Tim Richmond, and Rusty Wallace also showed in the top 14.)

The Parsons–Elliott duo did not win the Buck contest, and, all said and done, that chapter seemed to be closed. The Mercury sat in the garage for a month, with Mell-Gear still on its flanks, before the next planned race, at 1.5-mile Atlanta on November 2. Harry Melling had offered no more money, but rather than repaint the car, George and crew traveled south to Atlanta International Raceway with the ID intact.

"We were ready to go out of the racing business," George explained some time afterward. "The automobile business was bad, but we still had the dealership, and Dan was working there. We felt we could put the other two boys there and make a living, but really, we had no immediate plans."

With his life on the line, Bill qualified second for the 500-miler, his first-ever front-row start. His clutch burned out early, and he, Ernie, and the lads spent almost 60 laps changing it out. Although Elliott was running at leaders' pace at the finish, he ended up 18th, the last survivor at the flag.

But all was not yet lost. Bill's front-row qualifying effort had drawn favorable scrutiny from the hometown media, which, incidentally, rubbed against Harry Melling and Mell-Gear. Just as the Elliotts were packing to head home for good, word came from Melling that he would back the team for up to $35,000 the following season, in up to 12 races.

Along the road to the top in NASCAR are the bones of many who missed the one big break, or getting it, failed to capitalize. Bless the hearts of Tommy Gale, Joe Millikan, Baxter Price, Jim Vandiver, and Dave Watson—all now names on the bookshelf of time.

In the chilly gloaming of a fall afternoon at Atlanta, Bill Elliott and crew won a second chance at bat, and they swung for the fence.

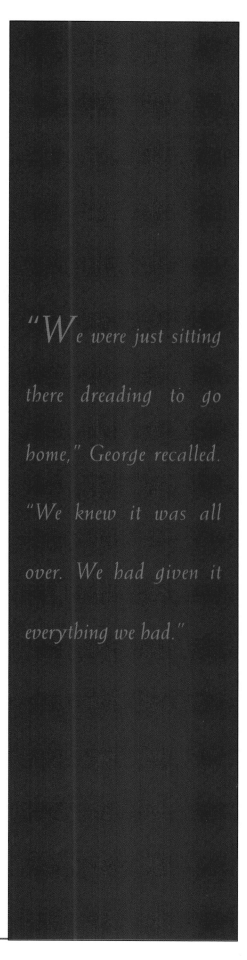

"We were just sitting there dreading to go home," George recalled. "We knew it was all over. We had given it everything we had."

Bill Begins His Ascent to the Top

Harry Melling's tithe for 1981 marked a business decision for the Melling companies and a bridge over troubled waters for the Elliott family—and little more. Bill and Ernie, increasingly wise to the ways of major-league racing, sank most of that little bundle into a new chassis from the manufactory of Banjo Matthews, then the top car builder in the sport, and the rest of it into reconstructing the Mercury around the new rules requirements.

Both cars were skinned as Thunderbirds—the old, boxy 'Bird—in large part because of the family's stubborn devotion to Ford. At Atlanta in March, where Elliott opened his limited 1981 campaign (starting 10th and finishing ninth), only five other Fords had been entered in the 42-car field. Benny Parsons, driving for Bud Moore, finished fifth. Old pal Jody Ridley, driving for Junie Donlavey, was sixth. Tommy Gale came in 18th, and Neil Bonnett, chauffeur for the Wood Brothers, broke and was 28th. Everyone else drove General Motors products, with the exception of Buddy Arrington, in a privateer Dodge.

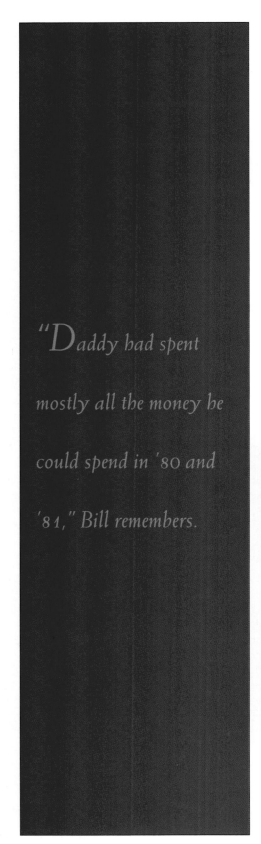

"Daddy had spent mostly all the money he could spend in '80 and '81," Bill remembers.

Hanging in with Ford meant driving a shoe box on wheels compared to the more popular Buicks back in the early 1980s. Despite the obvious disadvantage, Bill managed to hold his own against the top teams. While the car looked the same for several years, Bill's boyish facial features gradually grew into the handsome young man that helped win over the fans.

This *was* the GM era in NASCAR, before aero-matching. The sport, very slowly, was emerging from its 1970s dark ages, the grim period following the manufacturer pull-outs and the fuel crisis. NASCAR's foundation stone through this time was the cheap and plentiful GM small-block V8, the 350, which showed unmatched performance and reliability, with very little aftermarket tinkering.

Ford also had an engine to fit the formula, its strong but fragile 351. The surviving Ford loyalists, especially Moore, had made progress with the 351's fragile top-end package through the late 1970s and early 1980s, with next-to-no factory support, although problems persisted, especially in overheating and cylinder-head cracking. Meanwhile, down in Dawsonville, Georgia, a young perfectionist named Ernie Elliott was finding solutions on his own.

"I think everybody had got a little complacent in the racing world," Ernie recalls. "The competition wasn't like it is today, and I think we came in at a time when we had good power and not too many people were running Fords, other than Bud and Leonard [Wood] and that crowd. We were able to put it all together."

A hint of that aptitude came in the Elliotts' second try that season, at Darlington in April. Bill raised the size of headlines a few points by winning the first pole of his career with a lap of the ancient 1.366-mile track in just under 32 seconds (153.896 miles per hour). That news shook the flatlands of eastern South Carolina—although the present standard has risen to well over 170. He went on to finish fourth in Sunday's 500-miler.

Darlington, widely considered one of the toughest courses to race on the NASCAR circuit, served as a launching pad for Bill's budding career. He won four of his five Darlington poles and four of his five Darlington races through 1988, as his

Following a path previously laid by the Petty family, Bill and his brothers were the key figures in building a successful race team. Ernie (above) was the team leader and was in charge of the engines, while Dan (left) changed tires on race day and was responsible for the transmissions and rear ends. Bill assisted wherever necessary and was somewhat of a specialist in chassis.

success built to a peak. Darlington separates the racers from the drivers, allowing seat skill to rise to the top. If nothing else, Darlington put Bill's talents in a frame, at least to wiser observers.

Each achievement was a step forward, although that was hard to see from the inside, at times. At Talladega in May, for example, Elliott got tangled in a second-lap wreck, which also took out Harry Gant, Benny Parsons, and Richard Petty. At Charlotte, his clutch wore through, leaving him 40th in a very fast field. At Michigan (15 miles from Melling's home base in Jackson) in June, Bill crashed and finished 35th. The luck improved some through late summer and fall, and the team closed with a sixth-place, lead-lap finish at Atlanta. The season count showed seven top 10s in 13 tries and $70,320 in official pay—hardly enough to cover the bills.

"Daddy had spent mostly all the money he could spend in '80 and '81," Bill remembers. "I think '81 about did us in as far as spending money, and we didn't spend much."

Once again, though, circumstances began to combine in the Elliotts' favor, thanks in part to performance, and thanks in part to old friends. Veteran champion Parsons, who had taken Bill under his guidance in the late 1970s, had decided to step away from full-time racing. Bud Moore, Benny's car owner, had carried Harry Melling's top dollars through 1981, with Melling Tool on the quarter panels.

Dale Earnhardt, meanwhile, had endured some sudden and unpleasant changes mid-year, when Kentucky coal baron J.D. Stacy bought the Rod Osterlund team out from under him. Earnhardt had a firm sponsorship commitment from Wrangler Jeans; he shopped that to Moore, and a deal was made, which played well for just about everyone, Parsons teaming for a limited 1982 schedule with Harry Ranier.

The last piece of the puzzle fell into place when, at the suggestion of old Michigan friends Jim and Jan Knutson, Melling and the Elliotts decided to sit down and talk. Parsons, meanwhile, also had recommended that Harry consider the Elliotts for patronage in the next campaign.

What followed may not have been simple, but it happened quickly. "We flew up [to Michigan] one morning and flew back that night," Bill recalls. "We sat down with Harry in his office. Ernie did all the talking. I just sat there with my mouth hanging open."

Melling agreed not only to sponsor the team, but to take it over. Late in 1981, the home-grown family team from north Georgia became Melling Racing. The relationship, all in all over the long haul, was easy, friendly, and beneficial. Melling ran the business side from Michigan, leaving the Elliotts to direct racing from Dawsonville.

Harry Melling (left) became more than just a sponsor when he bought ownership of the Elliott family team. Harry was easily recognized with his ever-present cigar. Few photos exist without it.

"We just sent the bills up there and they paid them," Bill says with a shrug. "But I felt like we were spending the money as if it was our money. I don't think Harry ever argued with the way we tried to treat him.

"Here we had an operation in Dawsonville, and he was in Jackson, Michigan. We really didn't have an authority sitting there with a thumb over us saying you can't buy this or can't buy that. The trust between us was pretty whole-hearted. I feel like through the whole period of time I drove for Harry Melling, we never really messed with each other at all. We were able to perform for him, also. We won him races."

That did not happen right away. Despite the team's new name, it remained, fundamentally, the quietly diligent family team from some place in Georgia, with Ernie, Bill, and Dan doing much of the work themselves in their 5,000-square-foot building near home.

What began to open eyes was that the Elliott boys persisted in running Fords, with little or no factory support. Ford was only indirectly involved *anywhere* in NASCAR at the time. General Motors makes had come to dominate Winston Cup in the early 1980s, with Buick-bodied cars the top choice. But the Elliotts not only stuck with Fords, they made them work.

As Melling Racing, the Elliotts were able to expand their schedule, running 21 of the 30 races in 1982. Bill opened with a surprising fifth place at the Daytona 500, two laps behind winner Bobby Allison. He backed that up with third place at Darlington, and then, on a hot afternoon in Charlotte, he came *this* close to winning the World 600, falling two lengths short of Neil Bonnett.

His growing confidence showed in his post-race remarks (after being treated for effects of the heat).

Bill drove the boxy T-bird to numerous top fives, including several second places while running partial seasons in 1981 and 1982.

"If I had it to do over," he said at the time, "I'd make my move on Neil earlier. I made it on the last lap [through the final corner] and didn't get it. I should have tried on the next-to-last lap. I worked my butt off, but I finished second, and I can think of a million things I should have done."

Momentum built as the Elliotts added second places in two more high-profile events, the Firecracker at Daytona in July (to Allison) and the National 500 at Charlotte in October. He also claimed his second career pole, at Michigan's Champion 400, with a speed of 162.995 mph.

By the end of 1982, the Elliotts had built a pretty nice pile of achievements: the pole, eight top fives in 21 tries, and 14th in laps led (despite running very few short-track races). Just as rewarding, the team, with Ernie designated as crew chief, won the season-long Ingersoll-Rand crew competition, outscoring the likes of champion Jeff Hammond, Kirk Shelmerdine, and Gary Nelson.

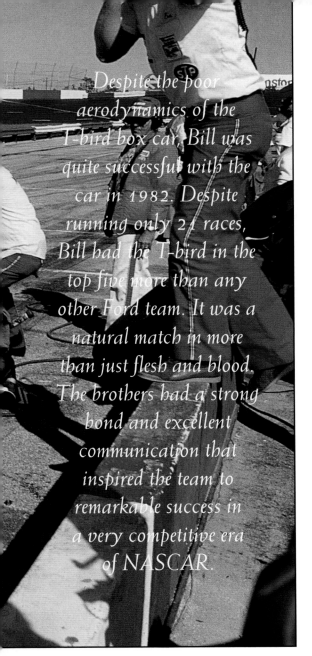

Despite the poor aerodynamics of the T-bird box car, Bill was quite successful with the car in 1982. Despite running only 21 races, Bill had the T-bird in the top five more than any other Ford team. It was a natural match in more than just flesh and blood. The brothers had a strong bond and excellent communication that inspired the team to remarkable success in a very competitive era of NASCAR.

"I guess when we came along, we looked at things a little differently, and we were able to make everybody else go to work," Bill says. "We weren't in the Charlotte clique. They didn't know what we were doing, and we were kind of in our own little world. They didn't know what we had."

The gradual curve of progress continued into 1983, and Bill and the team capitalized. They ran the full schedule for the first time, all 30 races, and appeared in the points top 20 for the first time—in third place, behind Bobby Allison and Darrell Waltrip but ahead of Richard Petty, Harry Gant, and Dale Earnhardt. Best of all, Bill notched his first career victory at, of all places, the Riverside, California, road course on the last Sunday of the season.

The year began with a bang, Elliott again finishing second (to Cale Yarborough), sixth the following week in his first visit to Richmond, then second again at Rockingham. He came to the summer break with six top fives in 15 events, including a second place in the June race at the 2.62-mile Riverside course. Down the stretch, he added third at Michigan (rapidly becoming his favorite track), second in Darlington's Southern 500, and a fourth at Richmond—so much for the myth that Bill couldn't run on short tracks.

Anticipation built—eighth place at Charlotte, sixth at Atlanta—to the long haul to California. Bill qualified 10th, amid a tense war of words among the top two points contenders, leader Allison and jabbering Waltrip. Waltrip led the most laps, and he and Richmond clearly had the cars to beat toward the end.

Suddenly, Waltrip and Richmond collided off course, giving the lead to Benny Parsons. Elliott shot by Parsons three laps later, and five laps later, there in the scrubby desert, it began to rain. Elliott had taken his first NASCAR victory, not at Daytona or Atlanta or Michigan, but on a road course.

"I don't think we planned for [Riverside] any different," Bill says. "We'd been running more competitively every time out, and we prepared for there no different than for anywhere else.

"It was just a situation, Darrell and Tim Richmond probably had the best cars there, they ended up taking each other out there in turn 9. That left Benny and myself, and I knew the weather was looking marginal. I made a move on him in turn 9, then it started raining.

"There you go . . ."

Despite the emerging success in 1983, Harry Melling was not in a position to stretch his company's racing budget further. To take the next step, the team would need additional backing. Toward the end of 1983, Coors Brewing Company approached the Elliotts, and the deal was made to bring team and brand together for 1984.

Big corporate sponsorship was not unknown in 1983. Pepsi/Gatorade, STP, Wrangler Jeans, and Skoal were among the products represented. Much of the national-brand marketing, though, seemed to concern beer. Tim Richmond carried Old Milwaukee, Terry Labonte Budweiser, and Bobby Allison had Miller High Life. The Elliotts, with their rush to the top, had created an opportunity for the Coors Company, and Coors had the foresight to seize it.

Bill Elliott

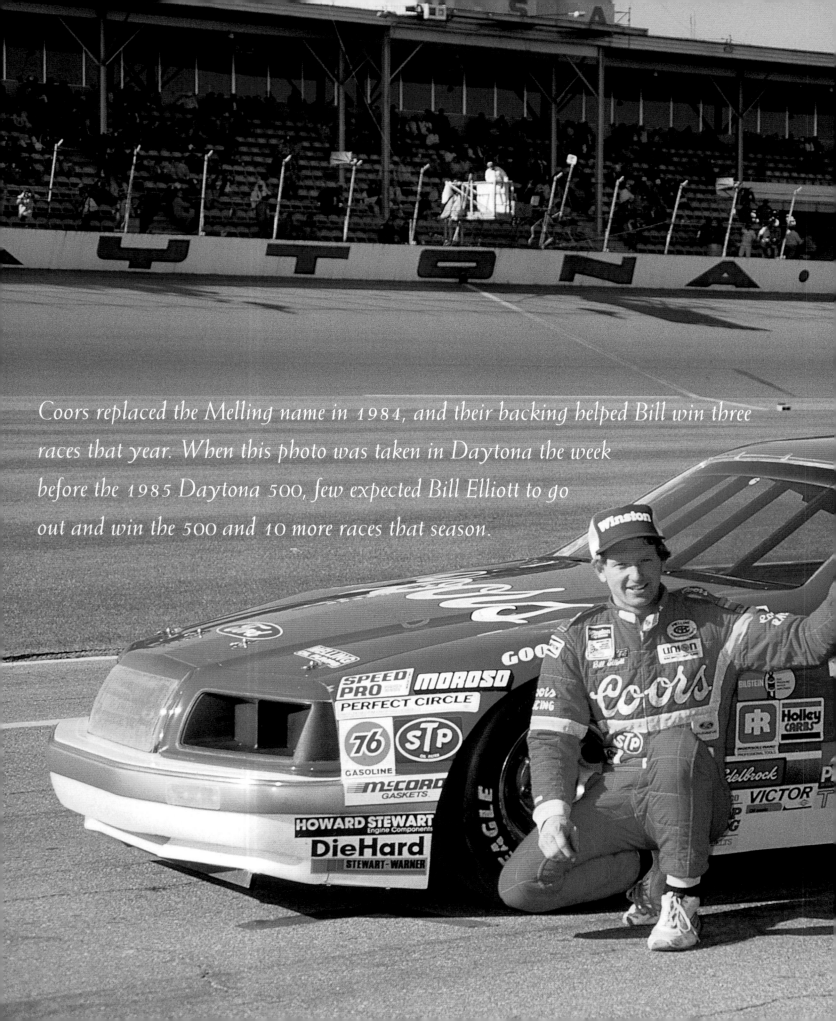

Coors replaced the Melling name in 1984, and their backing helped Bill win three races that year. When this photo was taken in Daytona the week before the 1985 Daytona 500, few expected Bill Elliott to go out and win the 500 and 10 more races that season.

In October 1982, Bill finished second to Harry Gant at Charlotte. Harry was famous for finishing second numerous times until he finally won two races that year. Bill appeared to inherit that second place routine.

Melling Racing and the Elliotts now were full-fledged members of an exclusive club—now among the top 10 funded teams in the sport. How it all built to be still mystifies the boys from north Georgia. They'd just come to race. Now they—and NASCAR—began to find themselves part of a larger corporate architecture.

Bill, Ernie, and Dan also found themselves on the fast track to the top in 1984.

A major element, aside from the sponsorship, was the arrival late in 1983 of Ford's redesigned Thunderbird. The new model, replacing the slab-sided heavyweights of previous seasons, was low, sleek, and aerodynamic.

Ernie always had made good, homegrown power, beginning with equipment George Elliott had bought for the speed shop in the late 1960s. Some complained about the durability of the Ford 351 engine, with only one engine failure through all of 1983.

Dan was a perfectionist with gears and transmissions, evident in the team's Riverside victory. Together, the three took a pretty nice little piece and turned it into the fastest hot rod in America.

The team, meanwhile, expanded, doubling the size of its shop to 10,000 square feet ("some people's motor coaches are bigger than that these days," Bill says with a laugh) and hiring some skilled help.

"We kind of had a feel for where we were going, and we were getting our feet wet everywhere we went," Bill recalls of his second full season. "We were making good racing decisions, gaining experience, our stuff was holding together, and we had a good car."

In 1984, thus armed, what had been a distant star began to glow brightly, and that season set the stage for the grand illumination that followed in 1985. He needed 15 races to get his first victory that season (at Michigan, where he went on to win six of the next eight, including four in a row). But he closed with a rush, winning at Charlotte and Rockingham, where he beat Harry Gant by a foot in a dash to the line.

The season totals included $660,226 in prize money, four poles, seven outside poles, a track record at Michigan, third place in points once again, and Bill's first most popular driver honor. It was altogether a satisfying season, and the Elliotts had reasons to count their blessings.

Then time and fortune conspired to change the Elliotts lives forever, in ways they never could have imagined.

At the NASCAR Winston Cup banquet in New York in December, series sponsor R.J. Reynolds Tobacco announced that, in 1985, it would (a) pay the champion $1 million, and (b) present a special bonus of $1 million to a driver who could win

Bill was not afraid to get his hands dirty. He was in the garage alongside his teammates to get the job done.

The good ole boys were not paid anything for helping us for a long time, just food and lodging at races which was sometimes six or seven to a room. Finally they were paid $25 per day sometime around the early eighties, then $50. When Coors took over it was $100 per day at the races. Steve Reagan worked with Ernie in the engine shop. Ernie was paid $50,000 a year and Steve was somewhere in the $20,000's. We were rich!

From left to right: *Steve Reagan, Clinton Chumbley, Loyal Wilson, Dan Elliott, Michael Hill, Bill Brookhardt; Standing: Ernie Elliott.*

three of the sport's four majors: Daytona 500, Winston 500, World 600, and Southern 500. That had not been accomplished in the sport's modern era.

Despite the stumble at Charlotte, Elliott built a legend through the summer, despite NASCAR's efforts to bring Bill back into the barn. It ordered roofline modifications to bring the Ford and General Motors cars equal, and it trimmed carburetor-bore size on the Fords by a quarter-inch. NASCAR's dilemma, of course, was the same as it confronted 12 years later with Jeff Gordon and Hendrick Motorsports: One car of one make was so much better than *every* car on the track that it was difficult to square up the field by changing the rules for a car brand.

That mattered little. Elliott swept mid-year races at both Michigan and Pocono, bringing his season wins total to nine. Labor Day loomed, with the Southern 500 at Darlington and the last shot at Winston's million bucks.

Unlike at Charlotte, the Elliotts came prepared, both mentally and logistically. RJR and the team managed the media properly, and South Carolina state troopers took posts at the Elliotts' garage stall to keep the surging mob under control, to allow Bill and his brothers to prepare the cars.

"Darlington was really easy, compared to Charlotte," he remembers. "Darlington wasn't hard at all. We had everything regimented. You went in and did your press conference, then you went back and worked on the race car. Charlotte was just a feeding frenzy."

Bill won the pole at 156.641 mph, with childhood hero David Pearson outside-front. The show was Elliott at his classic best, conserving the car and tires, dodging hazards (including a flying hood from Tim Richmond's car), and crossing the finish line, incredibly, the winner of the inaugural Winston Million Dollars.

"To come down there and sit on the pole and do it was pretty incredible," Elliott says in the plainest way he can say it. "We'd had a lot of months to prepare for it, we brought back the car I won with in the spring, and I think we did an excellent job of handling the pressure. It wasn't necessarily the best car all day long, but we won the race. That's all that counted."

RJR chief Jerry Long smiled and inscribed the check for $1 million, made out to Bill Elliott. Bill laughs now at the idea of $1 million being small change in the present environment.

"By the time Harry got his portion and Uncle got his . . ." he says with a shrug. "The team got a substantial amount, so it was pretty broken up. I probably ended up with like $75,000, and back then I was paying for all the facilities in Dawsonville."

In 1983, T-bird introduced a streamlined body for the car and many teams used both body styles. The old boxy car was still used for certain short tracks and the road course. At Riverside, under dark skies, Bill won his first Winston Cup race and his only Winston Cup victory on a road course in the old shoe box.

Almost lost in the uproar was the fact that Elliott had led in points all season, with two-time champion Darrell Waltrip hanging 100 to 200 points behind most of the way. With the million paid, the light and heat turned to the championship race, with Bill once again at the center of the spotlit square.

Luck turned against the Elliotts at Richmond, Dover, and Martinsville, and Waltrip closed, cutting the gap from 206 points to 23 in a month. At North Wilkesboro, as the leaves turned, the Ford's flywheel shed teeth. Elliott finished 30th, handing the lead to Waltrip.

Some believe the Elliotts suffered a letdown after the million. Bill denied that. "The points race is a different situation," he said at the time. "With what I've been through this year, there couldn't be any more pressure."

Others believe mouthy Waltrip turned up the wick on Elliott, pressing the team into mistakes. That's kind of silly, when you think about it. "Darrell never bothered me," he says. "We were all to ourselves."

The points gap stayed agonizingly close down the stretch, with Elliott never trailing by more than 20 through his last victory of the season, at Atlanta. In the finale at Riverside, however, a broken shifter left him in 30th. Waltrip finished seventh and won his third Winston Cup in five years.

The greatest season in NASCAR history thus finished without a clean sweep. Bill had won everything else—11 poles, 11 races, $1 million—but the championship, the logical reward for a great performance, slipped away down the stretch.

Still, Elliott has no regrets.

"I look at the whole scenario," he says. "We survived a lot of different stuff throughout the year. The proudest part of the whole deal was we did it on our own. It was all our little deal. In '85, there were 12 people at that dang shop, running on half a million dollars, at the most. We came in, we started with nothing, we grew and built what we had, and we won races that way.

"It about killed us."

Performance breeds expectation, and expectations were high for the Elliotts heading into 1986. They'd done everything in 1985 except win the championship, and their rapid moon shot from 1983 through 1985 had set the pieces on the board.

For 10 seasons, from 1976 to 1985, the Elliotts had set their sights upward, and despite the long hours, penny counting, and hardships, they'd seen the bright hope at the end of the run. In 1986, they began to see what was on the other side of the hill.

It started in January. Ernie began feeling draggy, as if he had the flu. By early February, the diagnosis was more serious—mononucleosis, a wearing ailment that normally affects younger people. It didn't knock Ernie out of action, but it limited his meticulous (some say obsessive) work with the engines and the team. Dan, meanwhile, took over engine prep and strategy in the pits.

Bill won the pole for the Daytona 500, just missing his track record, and again he knocked out a win in his qualifier. He was running top five in the 500 when disaster struck, a multicar pileup that left him patching up his car in the pits.

Results were fair through April, and Elliott set yet another record at Talladega in May, flying by the clock at 212.229 mph—still the second-fastest official lap in NASCAR history. Bill led 116 of the 188 laps, but the engine quit 13 laps from the end. What had been totally right in 1985 was a shade short of right in 1986.

Michigan, home away from home, turned out to be salvation. Elliott won both races at the 2-mile track, his only two victories of the season, and he slumped to ninth in points by season's end. It wasn't a bad year, but in comparison with 1985, it was a puzzle.

Ernie was back to full strength in 1987, and the team aimed for the run up the next hill. One big difference this time around, however, was that the Elliott team had yielded to pressure on two fronts. First, the demands on workaholic Ernie had become too great; the group needed a crew chief as crew chief, period. Second, to win a championship, a team needed a steady short-track program, and the Elliotts admitted theirs fell short.

To fill in those blanks, the Elliotts brought in Ivan Baldwin, West Coast short-tracker and car-builder, as designated chief. Baldwin thus became the first non-family team leader.

A jubilant Bill Elliott proudly shows off his damp trophy for his first win. Sporting a Coors hat, he gave a preview of his new look for 1984.

Western
500

Coors
RACING TEAM

WESTERN
Winston
500

MELLING
Performance Parts

STP

Bill
Elliott

MELLING
Performance Parts

UNION 76

GOOD YEAR

Motorcraft Ford

CHAMPION

MONROE

SIMPSON
SAFETY EQUIPMENT

With the support and resources of a major sponsor, Bill and his team got the backing they needed to reach the pinnacle of NASCAR Winston Cup Racing.

The 1987 season began much as 1985 had, with Elliott smashing the pole record at Daytona, his 210.364-mph lap beating his previous standard by a full five mph. He came in second to surprising Ken Schrader in his Thursday heat, then won the 500 when leader Geoff Bodine ran out of gas a few laps from the finish.

What the Elliotts could not have anticipated was the growing maturity of Dale Earnhardt and his Richard Childress–owned team. Earnhardt and mates put together a season almost as extraordinary as Elliott's 1985, without the groundbreaking enhancement of RJR's million bucks. Earnhardt won 11 races (although only one pole) and finished with a 488-point lead over Elliott—the largest margin to that time under the current marking system.

Bill Elliott

Elliott, more quietly, racked up his own set of achievements, including NASCAR's all-time, one-lap speed record—the incredible 212.809-mph qualifying run at Talladega that May. Given that NASCAR now restricts speeds at its two biggest tracks, that's a record not likely to change.

Ironically, the Sunday following was the day NASCAR's speed chase came to an end. With Elliott and young hot-shot Davey Allison dueling for the lead in the Winston 500, the car of Davey's father, legendary Bobby Allison, left the ground off turn 4 and tore into the catch fence. Thanks to recently installed, reinforcing back-up cables, the fence held, preventing what could have been terrible loss of life. After a two-hour delay for repairs to the fence, the race resumed. When Elliott's engine gagged 28 laps from the finish, Davey Allison outran Terry Labonte to become the sport's newest winner.

Meanwhile, confrontation had been brewing between roughneck Earnhardt, then just flexing his muscles, and calculating Elliott, whom Earnhardt had been needling since Daytona. The climax came at The Winston, NASCAR's unofficial all-star race at Charlotte in May, with bystander Geoff Bodine caught in the middle.

Earnhardt prevailed with his legendary "Pass in the Grass" down the front stretch, but the bust-up over the final couple of laps spilled over into the pits, with Elliott's red-clad crewmen facing off with Earnhardt's men in black. Fortunately, tempers cooled to the sizzling point, fines were handed out, and no wrenches were thrown.

Elliott's chase for the championship in 1987 developed too late to do him any good, at least for 1987. He did not win again until Talladega in July, then followed up by outrunning Earnhardt at Michigan in August. He finished with a rush, winning at Charlotte, Rockingham (where Earnhardt clinched), and in the finale at Atlanta.

Garry Hill, a well-known artist in racing circles, produced this now-famous piece of art, Dale Earnhardt's legendary "Pass in the Grass."

The momentum was up heading into 1988. The team had given up on its Ivan Baldwin experiment, although Bill does not fault Baldwin. He also disagrees with the idea that anyone outside the family somehow did not fit in.

"It was getting beyond me doing everything I had to do," he remembers. "I'd won a number of races and done a lot of stuff, and the demands on me were so great, I was trying to do everything, and it was tough.

"Ivan was a totally different person anyway. I love Ivan to death, but he was very opinionated and used to running his own business. He did a lot of good stuff for us, but I think he didn't like living in Dawsonville. He wanted to be in Charlotte."

So Ernie was back in charge, basically, for 1988, the year the Elliotts cleared the final hump, the NASCAR Winston Cup championship.

The championship year may have been the Elliotts' finest, although not nearly as eye-catching and spectacular as 1985. For one thing, speed was no longer the story; in response to Allison's frightening crash at Talladega the previous year, NASCAR choked down the cars with restrictor plates, and Ken Schrader, now driving for Rick Hendrick, sputtered to the pole at 198.823 mph. Daytona's pole speed has not reached 200 since Elliott's last fast run, in 1987.

The plates changed the whole game. "It's like, NASCAR makes a rule change, whether it be engines, bodies, or whatever," Bill explains. "You've got a specific way you do something, so it might take away from a guy who's got a good setup and give it to a guy who's got a bad setup. In other words, his setup might work with a particular change, where your setup might not work with a particular change, like the engine combination and the rest of the deal.

"We were set up unrestricted, then the plates came in. Yeah, we won a restrictor-plate race at Daytona the Fourth of July in '88, started in the back and won the race. But the evolution was changing so fast, and NASCAR was changing so fast. . ."

Aside from the plates came a titanic tire war, which twisted the balances of power beyond recognition. Goodyear, supplier of tires to NASCAR for 20 years, had endured a hostile corporate takeover bid, and NASCAR, in attempting to protect its show, invited racing-tire manufacturer Hoosier to join up.

Consequences of the war did not show immediately at Daytona, where Bill finished 12th. On the handling tracks that followed, Richmond and Rockingham, Neil Bonnett, then driving for Rahmoc, took control with Hoosier rubber. Lake Speed, of all people, used Hoosiers for a remarkable victory at Darlington two weeks later.

The world would sit up and take notice of the young man from Georgia. With help from Coors and Harry Melling, Bill could stand shoulder to shoulder with the best like Darrell Waltrip (top right) and run door to door with the likes of David Pearson (top), Dale Earnhardt (right), and Tim Richmond (below).

After that first win in the rain at
Riverside, the family enjoyed three more
days in the sun with three victories
in 1984. This was only the beginning.
The best was yet to come!

Elliott scored a private triumph at Bristol in April, posting his first short-track victory by two lengths over Mark Martin. Still, it took Goodyear almost half the year to sort out its weapons in the war. The Elliotts, like most NASCAR team Goodyear loyalists, had to bide time. Bill gained in points by beating Hoosier-shod Morgan Shepherd at Dover in June, by nearly a lap.

From the time Bill and the Elliott team came of age in 1983, they had battled the best—Waltrip, Earnhardt, Allison. The challenger in 1988 turned out to be relative newcomer Rusty Wallace, driving for the slaphappy, long-shot Blue Max team.

Two victories in a row in the summer (Daytona, after starting 38th, and Pocono) made Bill a contender in one of the tightest, season-long points races in history. When Rusty flipped at Bristol, and Elliott followed with a dramatic victory at Darlington, Bill took the points lead.

Elliott gathered strength down the stretch, winning at Dover and surviving a three-race winning streak by Rusty into October. It all came down to the closing race at Atlanta, where Bill drove to 15th place—almost exactly what he needed to do with Wallace winning and leading the most laps. The final margin was 24 points.

He had done it. He and his family had done it. From a competitor's point of view, glamorous 1985 had been an education. In 1988, Bill, Ernie, and Dan put that education to work, picked through the odds, and won NASCAR racing's biggest prize, the Winston Cup.

"I was asked after the Atlanta race how this compares to our team in 1985, when we won 11 races, the Winston Million, and lost the Winston Cup title," Elliott said at the time. "There's no comparison."

Today, he is more reflective. "I'd say '88 was pretty much a blur from the standpoint of stating a year," he says. "It's just like I keep saying today, you can't go out there and worry about points. You have to go out there with the attitude that you're going to win the race and run the best you can, and the points are going to take care of themselves.

"That's what we did in '88. Rusty had me beat at Phoenix, then he crashed, and that put him out of the deal. At Atlanta, we had to finish 21st, that's all. Ernie and I, we did what we wanted to do. We went out, finished the race, finished where we needed to finish, and went home with the championship.

"It was all part of that growing equation. I think '88 just kind of put the icing on the cake. Everything was there. I never thought anything about 'this proves we've made it'."

The Elliotts made the top of the mountain in November 1988, and Bill, an accomplished skier, joked after the Atlanta finale that he planned to spend a week or two in Colorado, going downhill on the planks. The sense, after the long season and the championship, was more of relief than accomplishment.

"I'm going to crash and burn," Bill said with a little laugh.

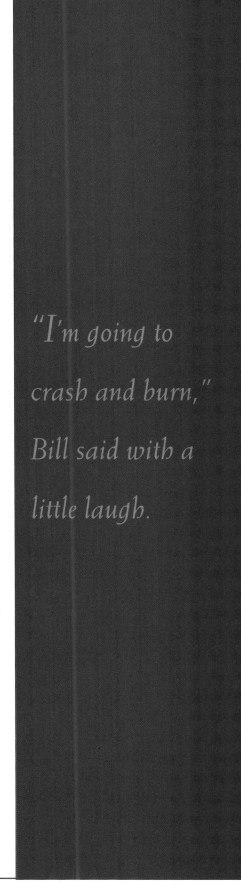

"I'm going to crash and burn," Bill said with a little laugh.

Bill Skyrockets to the Top in NASCAR Winston Cup

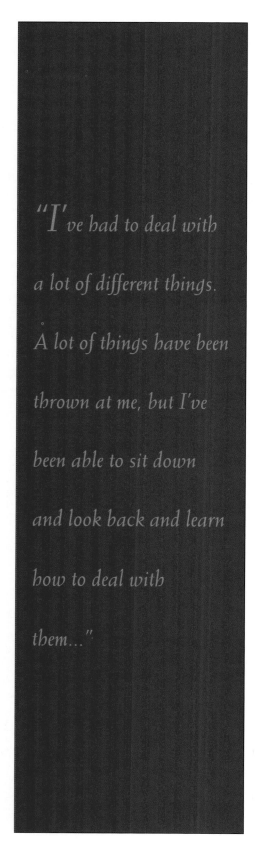

"I've had to deal with a lot of different things. A lot of things have been thrown at me, but I've been able to sit down and look back and learn how to deal with them..."

If drawn on a graph, the first 13 years of Bill Elliott's career would show a slow, steady rise through 1981, a rapid rise through 1985, a slight leveling in 1986 and 1987, then a spike to the peak in 1988. All throughout, the line shows progress, a steady move *up*.

After Bill's lucky 13th year, with the Winston Cup safely in the case, it's almost as though the bills came due. Chance and circumstance, which had worked in the Elliotts' favor for more than a decade (often in fantastic ways) seemed suddenly to conspire against them.

The 1989 season in ways paralleled 1986, a letdown year after a year of great accomplishment. He won three races (down from six), two poles (down from six), and recorded only 14 top 10s (down from 22). The money count, $854,570, was the team's lowest since 1984, in an era of rising purses and prizes.

The seeds of turmoil had been sown as far back as 1984, 1985, when the Elliotts were too busy to notice, too wrapped up in their racing. The stock-car racing game had changed faster than just about anyone could see, and the Elliotts were caught right up in the middle of it.

"Because I grew up in a small town, I was a product of the environment I grew up in, and I can't take that away," Bill said in an interview. "In '85, and I'll just lay it out on the table, I couldn't face a lot of things, I couldn't deal with it. Too many things came my way, and I just could not deal with it—personally, emotionally, so on and so forth.

"I've had to deal with a lot of different things. A lot of things have been thrown at me, but I've been able to sit down and look back and learn how to deal with them. It's taken me several years to do it, but I feel like I'm a 100 percent better person than I was six months ago or a year ago or two years ago.

"I never had *time* to mature. Too many things were going on. And I think I sat down one day and said, 'What does Bill Elliott want person-

There is no better way to begin a new season in NASCAR Winston Cup than by winning the prestigious Daytona 500. Note his daughter Starr, wearing Bill's helmet.

AYTONA
inston Cu
DAYTONA 500
HARLEY EARL AWARD
DAYTONA 500
1985 WINNER
THE WORLD CENTER OF RACING
Coors
Bill Elliott
UNION 76
BILSTEIN
SIMPSON
Coors
MELLI
Bill
1985

ally?' I started putting everything together after '86, '87, and it's been more or less a building process.

"It seems like I spend most of my time putting out fires, just addressing little old problems that become big problems. And it's day-in, day-out. It just seems everywhere you go it's always something you're having to put out, and it takes away from the racing side of the deal. If you can keep that stuff to a constant roar, where it's not blown out of shape, you can keep control."

In that respect, Bill was challenged to the limit, in public and in private, through 1989 and 1990. The challenges began the previous fall, when Ford unveiled some fairly serious styling changes to the Thunderbird for 1989, sending the Elliotts back to the aerodynamic drawing board. Then, at Daytona in February, disaster struck.

The tire war between Goodyear and Hoosier, which developed through 1988, brought an aggressive response from Goodyear in 1989, the belted "radial" tire. In the long run, the radial turned out to be an improvement, more cut-proof and predictable. In the short run, however, the radial felt different and drove different. That changed the tactics and set-up strategies of many veteran racers, who had been more accustomed to the flexy bias-ply.

On top of it all, the radial just wasn't ready for Daytona, and the first victim was Bill Elliott. In practice the week before the main event, one of the new tires came apart on Elliott's car, and Bill smashed into the concrete, breaking his left wrist.

With a cast on his arm, Bill still managed to qualify respectably, with anticipation of turning the car over to old neighbor Jody Ridley at the first chance in the race. Pole day brought a characteristic comment for Bill, about driving one-handed: "It's just like going down the road eating a hamburger," he said matter-of-factly.

In the inaugural year of the Winston million, Bill handily won the necessary three of the top five races that season. He made it look so easy and yet no other driver accomplished that feat under the original format.

Ridley, too, had trouble in the main event, hitting the wall in the first turn after completing just 72 laps. The team limped out of Florida with a 31st-place finish, and a long way to go.

It took until Charlotte in May, where Elliott finished fifth, for the team to find its feet; in fact, Bill did not lead a single lap until Sears Point in June, where he finished third. Michigan and Pocono, as always, brought saving grace, with wins in June and July, and Bill finished strong with a stout run to victory at Phoenix in October.

He finished sixth in points. It was a good year, but not an Elliott year.

Matters turned dark on the home front as well. Bill's relationship with his wife of 12 years, Martha, was on the rocks. They'd been married when Bill was 21, and the stress of change was just too much.

"I was young," he recalls, shaking his head. "I thought [getting married] was the thing to do, and I did it. Looking back on it, I was just too young. And I was so into racing. All I thought about was racing, and I

The 1980s saw quite a rivalry between two of NASCAR's most liked drivers. Dale Ernhardt and Bill Elliott (below) were immensely popular with the fans. They seemed to inherit the adoration that was passed on by number 43 Richard Petty (above) when his career began to fade. Bill looks just as comfortable in an Indy car as he is shown here trying out one of Chip Ganassi's Indy cars in 1991 at Michigan (left).

never thought about anything else. It just engulfs you.

"It's a hard thing to deal with, to make the decision whether to stay, go, whatever. It's sad. People go their separate ways, and you just can't make things work. A lot of things happened there. You take it a day at a time and a step at a time. You can't quit. You've got to keep digging."

Another blow fell late in the year when Mildred Elliott, beloved mother of the brothers, suffered a stroke. Mrs. Elliott was not debilitated, but the consequences were lasting. The winter of 1989–90 was a trying time for Bill Elliott.

The 1990 season started out well enough, with a third at Daytona, as leader Dale Earnhardt blew a tire on the last corner, and a fourth at Richmond. From there, however, results fell off the table to midseason. With the exception of the pole at Talladega in April and second place at Charlotte in May, Bill did not show a top five until back-to-back seconds at Pocono and Michigan deep into summer.

The World's Fastest Race Car

Filling in for brother Ernie during his illness, Dan (right) helped Bill put the Coors T-bird (left) in the record book with the fastest speeds ever made by a race car at Talladega. The 212.229 mph they accomplished in 1986 was broken the next year with a 212.809 mph.

(Left) Driving the world's fastest super-speedway car, Bill drove his car into victory lane at Daytona and Talladega more often than the rest of the field in the mid-1980s. (Bottom) 1988 saw Bill Elliott finally drive to the front of the pack and stay there until season's end.

The biggest challenge to Bill's championship drive in 1988 came from a young and aggressive Rusty Wallace.

Elliott finally won, at Dover in September, from the pole, and results were encouraging down the stretch, with fourth at North Wilkesboro, second at Rockingham, fifth at Phoenix. Then, in the finale at Atlanta, the hammer dropped again.

Racing is a sport in which men risk their lives. Every effort is made to protect the drivers from danger. The unsung heroes, and the ones who routinely court danger, are the pit workers. By 1990, pit work, increasingly the difference between winning and losing, had become the most dangerous job of all.

Kirk Shelmerdine, hall-of-fame crew chief for Dale Earnhardt, said once that "we make our living running out in front of cars at 100 mph. That's not too smart." This was in the days before pit-road speed limits, before the requirement that the pace car slow the leader before caution stops.

Bill and crew had put together a potential winner at Atlanta, taking the lead from Earnhardt on lap 293 of 328. On lap 297, caution waved, and Elliott pitted for tires and fuel. As tire changer Mike Rich squatted next to the right rear, Ricky

Clinching the championship in the season finale at Atlanta gave the whole team and their families the opportunity to join the celebration in victory lane.

Rudd's car, entering the pits with locked brakes, careened into the side of Elliott's. Mike Rich, a neighbor of Bill's from Blairsville, Georgia, died later that night.

Compounding the tragedy, NASCAR black-flagged Elliott for damage during the remaining caution laps, and Bill had to return to the pits. What looked to be a win in the making ended up a 15th place, and with a good friend killed.

"That was a bad deal," says Elliott, who reserves a corner of the Elliott Museum in Dawsonville to commemorate Mike. "I don't know that anybody took it harder than anybody else. To have one of your friends get killed and still have to finish the race . . ."

By mid-1990, Elliott even had considered taking some time off, backing away from the pressure that his success had helped create. But, "you couldn't do that if you wanted to," he said at the time. "I think I've really got my act together—where I'm going, what I'm doing—if I can just make everything work.

"Where Winston Cup is going in the next five or six years, I don't know. If it continues to grow like it is today, we're all going to have to be helped to weather a lot of the things that have happened to me."

Bill Elliott

All the years of work and toil and triumphs finally culminated with the Elliott and Melling families taking their race car from the track to Park Avenue!

Caught on the hamster wheel, however, Elliott's 1991 saw the break-up continue. Within a week mid-year, he lost his mother and grandmother. Mildred Elliott had been in declining health since the winter of 1989, but the loss hit hard.

Racing results continued to slip. Elliott won just once, at Daytona in July, and he slumped to 12 top 10s, his fewest since 1982. As a result, Elliott finished 11th in points, his first time out of the top 10 since 1982.

In the midst of this scramble, car owner Harry Melling was having second thoughts, as was sponsor Coors, which had changed its racing colors from the familiar red to blue in 1991. The stable, benevolent relationship among the parties, which had brought benefits since 1983, became strained.

"At the end of '91, Coors decided to get out of racing," Elliott recalls. "Harry was at a crossroads, and he didn't know whether he wanted to continue or not. I didn't know where my future was. We might could have attracted something [sponsorship], but at that point in time, Harry wanted things a certain

way. Harry didn't want to take his name off the car, so it was hard to find people wanting to pay any kind of money and say, 'Oh, keep your name on the car'."

Changes piled up. Teams at the time were trying out different kinds of cars in response to radial tires, switching from rear-steer to front-steer, with deviations into drop-snout, three-quarter-snout—all kinds of oddities. Aerodynamics became increasingly important. Teams began to rely more on shock absorbers as a tuning tool.

"That was a whole different adjustment," Elliott says, "the more aerodynamic cars, just the way you looked at racing in general. Everybody was getting away from rear-steer stuff, and that's what I'd done all my driving in.

"A lot of the stuff now, you don't even run in the realm of reality of what we ran back in the early days. Then, you went to the shock truck, got four shocks, bolted them on your car. It wasn't like you had to have shock dynos and technicians and umpteen engineers just to do shocks."

All that, of course, turned one of the Elliotts' strengths into a weakness. In the 1980s, a bunch of boys from faraway Dawsonville, Georgia, could show up at races, secrets well concealed, and beat the best in the business. By the early 1990s, it became harder to attract top-dollar technicians to small-town Georgia from the Charlotte orbit. The Elliotts fell farther behind.

Amid the personal losses and professional turmoil came a great brightness. After his divorce from Martha, Bill became acquainted with Cindy Karam, a professional photographer. Their acquaintance grew into a relationship, which resulted in marriage during the 1992–93 off-season.

The pairing brought a balance to Bill's life. Bill and Cindy both were familiar with the racing life, its pitfalls and demands.

Teamwork has always been one of the strong points of Bill Elliott's operation. Here, Bill's pit crew works to get him back out on the track.

If 1989 was a downer after the peak of 1988, then 1990 was just plain dismal! Always risky and dangerous, an accident on pit road took the life of Bill's friend, Mike Rich (above, right).

"We were always pretty good friends," Bill says of his wife. "But it was pretty ironic. I thought us getting together would be like oil and water—we were just a lot different. She was pretty detailed and had her stuff together on that end, stuff that had to do with paperwork and organization, which is the least of what I like to do.

"We were able to, I think, help each other in a lot of ways. That's been a great part. She's been very good from the business side too, very good on a lot of the stuff I was very weak in."

NASCAR did not allow women and children in the garages until the 1980s, and the motor coaches, homes away from home in the racing infields, did not become standard equipment until the mid-1990s. In so many ways, the NASCAR environment is much more felicitous for Bill, Cindy, and children Brittany and Chase than it was for Martha and daughter Starr.

"I don't know if anybody really understands the stress and strain of what you go through," Bill says. "Today, as far as NASCAR's concerned, we've got the motor homes, got all this stuff, and it's more family-friendly. We've got MRO [Motor Racing Outreach], got people around you can turn to when you do have a problem. Back then, it was either figure it out yourself or whatever. And I think I've matured as a person a lot more."

Bill Elliott

The only real highlight of 1989 was Bill's win at Dover in September.

After sporting the color red for most of his career, Bill was suddenly blue. As it sometimes happens, sponsors in the final year of a contract will try something new or try to garner a little publicity for one of their other products while finishing out the original contract.

As the Melling/Coors relationship became unglued in 1991, Elliott was forced to a decision. Meanwhile, Junior Johnson, winner of six championships with Cale Yarborough and Darrell Waltrip, was nearing the end of his relations with driver Geoff Bodine.

The importance of Junior Johnson in NASCAR history cannot be overstated. Up-front descendant of North Carolina's moonshine legacy, Johnson had been a great racer in his own time, winning 50 races. A shrewd businessman and big thinker, Johnson also developed relationships with Winston, Coca-Cola, Chevrolet, and Budweiser—all major American brands— as well as a deep and abiding connection with NASCAR and the France family. Through the 1970s and 1980s, Junior, at his desk in Wilkes County, North Carolina, was a broker, a deal maker, a powerful man.

Junior knew talent, and Bill Elliott, assuming anyone could pry him loose, was a coveted commodity. It happened that Bill reached the end of his string—and Junior needed a first-rate driver—at about the same time.

There was one complication, at least from a publicity standpoint. Elliott had been Coors's front man for 10 years. Budweiser had been the sponsor of Johnson's number 11 even longer. Oddly, Elliott, who does not drink, was caught in the middle of the beer war. He reached agreement with Johnson in the summer of 1991 but could not say anything about it until New Year 1992.

There had been dream teams before, the most notable recent being Tide's assembly of Waltrip and crew chief Waddell Wilson with Hendrick Motorsports in 1987. In 1992, Johnson and Budweiser gathered up the

Bill's blue T-bird now advertised Coors Light and he managed to bring the car to victory lane in Daytona on a hot July weekend.

sport's most popular star, Elliott, with one of its most savvy and aggressive crew chiefs, Tim Brewer.

What happened to Harry Melling? Melling continued in racing on a limited schedule, mostly out of his own pocket, and kept the number 9. He stayed in the game until his sudden death in 1999, with a variety of drivers and sponsors. His son, Mark, took over the team after Harry's death and, in an oddly coincident parellel, joined Elliott in the move to Dodge for 2001.

In 1993, for the first time in 11 years—back to the pre–Harry Melling days—Bill failed to win a race, managing only six top fives, sixth in points, and less than a million dollars in race winnings. The previous winter, Johnson had handed off number 22, sponsor Maxwell House and Brewer to Bill Davis's team, making the jump to Winston Cup with Bobby

Technology and cash lead
to big changes in racing.
These good old boys in
Dawsonville, Georgia,
accomplished quite a lot.
But times were changing!

Making a major move in 1992 that surprised many observers, Bill Elliott left his famous Melling number 9 T-Bird and climbed into the equally famous number 11 (right). Not only was the change of teams quite surprising, but it also involved switching to competitive sponsor Budweiser!

(Bottom) The teaming of Junior Johnson and Bill Elliott appeared destined for success. Coming back from a dismal wreck in 1992's opening Daytona 500, the team went out and won the next four races. The phenomenal start slowed but the team managed to finish out the year with Bill's fifth win in the season finale at Atlanta (right). Joining him in victory lane at Atlanta (below) was his Dad George, Daughter Starr, and his bride-to-be, Cindy Karam.

Labonte. Mike Beam became Elliott's crew chief.

One important development had occurred, however: McDonald's had come aboard as sponsor of Johnson's second team, the number 27, with Hut Stricklin replacing Sterling Marlin. Stricklin also failed to win, as Johnson drew a blank for the first time since 1966.

Much had changed. NASCAR in 1992 forced all manufacturers to adopt a single factory pattern for cylinder heads, and Johnson's templates were, in effect, outlawed. Gary Nelson, meanwhile, had taken over as garage chief and was beginning to tinker with aerodynamics and matching of the cars.

"In the first part of the year, I hadn't worked with Mike in a long time," Elliott recalls. "We tried to change some things around, and I don't necessarily think we were working in the right direction. NASCAR changing things around sure didn't help nothing, and there again, they kept shaking things up, and just as we'd get a little better, it would get worse."

Change came again for tandem sponsor McDonald's, with Johnson replacing Stricklin with Jimmy Spencer. Spencer, one of the sport's colorful characters, wasn't quite the right fit either, although he won two races in 1994. Through the spring, however, Elliott learned that McDonald's might like to talk business. Bill's three-year term with Johnson was in its third year, and the uncertainty was wearing on him.

In association with Charles Hardy, an old business and racing associate of George Elliott, Bill began to form a new team back home in Dawsonville. With Melling still holding the number 9, the Elliott–Hardy team decided on number 94 in honor of nephew Casey Elliott, who had been stricken with cancer and his racing career no longer viable. The new team came out from wraps in January 1995 in the bright red and yellow of McDonald's, one of the world's most formidable marketing entities.

Once again, Bill Elliott was his own boss.

With a new body style for 1989, new radials from Goodyear and just plain old misfortune, Bill saw his 1988 high drop to a season that started off with a lot of frustration and a long wait before a return to victory lane.

He had left Johnson on somewhat of a high note. Even with his car overheating, Elliott roared from behind, passed leader Dale Earnhardt with 13 laps to go, and won Darlington's Southern 500 for the third time. That ended a 52-race losing streak, allowing him to mark up his 40th career victory.

"We finally fought back and started putting things back together at the end of '94," Bill remembers. " '93 was a struggle, but we were able to turn around and put things back together."

The new team, as might be expected, endured growing pains. He did not post a top 10 until finishing sixth at Talladega in April, and qualifying was middling through the first half, with Bill having to take a champion's exemption at Daytona in July. He began to see light two weeks later at Pocono, however, where he won the pole and finished fifth. At Talladega, he turned a champ provisional into another fifth place, and he finished up with the pole at Phoenix and a fourth place at Atlanta.

Teammate Hut Stricklin (above) and Bill discuss the number 27 McDonald's car after Bill took it out for a test drive. Bill's next teammate would be Jimmy Spencer (below) who took over for Stricklin. Bill himself took over the McDonald's colors in 1995.

Overall, the debut season was not bad. Bill notched four top fives and two poles and came home eighth in points. His official take for the season came to just a few dollars less than a million. There was reason to hope for better in 1996. The bright news in the off-season was the birth of son Chase in November.

Racing, however, continued to play cruel tricks. The team continued to sort through personnel, with Hardy leaving the partnership and Mike Beam rejoining Elliott as crew chief. But with the sport increasingly centered in the Charlotte area and with growing numbers of specialists required just to prepare the car and its parts, Bill found it difficult persuading people to move to Dawsonville, and to stay there.

"The hardest stuff is all the dramatic changes that have gone on throughout the years as far as technology is concerned," Bill says. "Used to be you had no engineers on your staff. You didn't even know what an engineer was, it was all trial and error. Then to get into the aerodynamic cars, radial tires, specialized shocks, this, that, everything else, man, it's just been wide-open."

Team stability, Bill says, is the key to success, and the McDonald's team seemed to go through some major change each year, almost from the start.

Despite the terrific debut in 1992, Bill had to look back over his association with Junior and Budweiser and felt a change in 1995 would be in his best interest.

Joining McDonald's and its successful marketing was the perfect match. The cleancut American icon and McDonald's family image made for a prosperous commodity that the company used extensively for advertising. Sporting various colors and schemes, the race car as well as Bill himself advertised whatever was deemed worthy, from Mac Tonight (above), Batman, the movie (left), and even Big Mac (bottom).

"You look at my deal since '89 or '90," he notes. "With Junior, it was stable that first year, then there was a lot of instability there until we finally got it built back. Then we turned around and started our own deal. We always had that instability.

"That's the key to this whole deal, being stable year-in and year-out. That's where the 24 car the last number of years, the 3 car, why they've always been so good. To me, that's as important as anything."

It didn't help at all that Bill was injured at Talladega in April, bringing the first extended absence of his career. His car went airborne and came down on all four wheels, with a force similar to dropping car and driver off a third-story balcony. Bill's left hip was fractured, and after surgery to insert a plate, he needed several weeks of therapy.

Nevertheless, as in 1995, the season started slowly. He earned seventh at Bristol, fourth at Charlotte, and eighth at Dover, aiming to gather momentum at the start of the summer stretch, and a strong, laps-led performance brought second place at Michigan in June, Bill's best of the season. He won the pole at Richmond in September.

The 1996 season just never got started. For the first time since 1980, Elliott failed to record a top five finish, and for the first time since 1983, he did not win a pole. Earnings for the season slumped to $716,506.

Order returned in 1997. Bill opened with a near-miss at the Daytona 500, which he led 17 laps late before the three Hendrick Motorsports cars, led by Jeff Gordon, drafted past him on lap 195. Elliott held on for fourth.

When all was counted, Elliott was eighth in points and seventh in miles led. Best of all, he had failed to complete only 281.38 of the nearly 13,000 total miles that season and had cashed in for better than $1.6 million, his best showing at the bank since 1992 with Johnson.

Meanwhile, Bill continued to anticipate what the business would need down the road. "It was hard to get people to come to Dawsonville. I couldn't keep my thumb on it every day, like Ernie and myself were able to do in the '80s, because it had grown in too many directions." So, in cooperation with Beam, from western North Carolina, he began to make plans for an ultra-modern shop near Statesville, North Carolina. Car service and preparation operations would be moved to the new complex in Statesville from Dawsonville, with engine work staying at Ernie's Dawsonville shop.

Meanwhile, owners such as Rick Hendrick, Robert Yates, Richard Childress, and Jack Roush had proved the multi-team concept, and Elliott saw the writing on the wall. He had been approached by old friend Dan Marino, former Miami Dolphins quarterback, who had backing from FirstPlus, a financial services company. Bill took on the added responsibility of setting up a second team for 1998 and hiring rookie driver Jerry Nadeau.

The new team was troubled from the start. The real trouble came when FirstPlus came up against cash-flow difficulties in late spring, and by July, Elliott–Marino Racing had folded. "The stock went *pfft*, then they pulled the plug on the sponsorship," Elliott recalls. "We all had good intentions, but it turned into a negative as far as the whole race team."

Year after year, Bill would go to New York and accept the "Most Popular Driver" Award from the National Motorsport Press Association.

Far worse were the personal losses. Ernie's son, Casey, had begun to show ability as a racer, running at some of the same Georgia tracks Bill had run as a youngster. Then, in 1993, at the age of 19, Casey was dignosed with cancer. He endured the travel and treatment and even managed to enter a Busch race or two before the disease worsened. Bill had become very close with his nephew by the time Casey died in January 1996 at 21.

"The family itself went through a lot," Bill says. "Mother had her long struggle in the early '90s, and there was Casey's deal in the mid-'90s and Dad's in the late '90s. There's always been something kind of chopping you down.

"Casey's was the hardest for me to accept. He was just a good kid. He had a lot of ability, and I think he would have done great. He'd already done a lot as young as he was.

Mike Beam rejoined Bill as his crew chief.

"I'll tell you what kind of person he was. It took everything you could do to go in there and see him and talk to him there toward the end. We used to try to get him feeling better, but when you walked out of there, he'd made *you* feel better. There ain't many people like that, especially in their early 20s, who can just sit there and face it."

Then, in 1998, George Elliott was diagnosed with a brain tumor. George Elliott, family patriarch, who had carried the family heart, soul, and dollars into racing in the first place, passed away in September 1998.

Racing, meanwhile, became more and more difficult for the independents, the owner-drivers. The two best were Elliott and Ricky Rudd, both of whom had launched out on their own at about the same time. By the beginning of 1999, both had come to see the writing on the wall. Neither had the finances, or the time, to do what it took to stay competitive.

"It's getting to the point where you've got to look at running a race team as virtually having no budget," Bill says. "You have to have deep enough pockets to keep throwing stuff at it. I think you're eventually going to see—NASCAR tries to keep it on a level playing field, but only the mega-teams are going to be the winning deals.

"It's about that way now. At first you could kind of subsidize it, but things have gotten so competitive you need to focus on what you're doing today and not worry about all this stuff going on around you.

" '97 was such a good year for us, '98 was mediocre, and '99 went in the toilet. It's discouraging, but I look at it from the standpoint of it's easier for me to accept because I've been on that side of the fence and I know what it takes to race, even running 15th."

That's about where Bill ran through most of 1999. The struggle had begun in 1998, when Bill slumped to 18th in points, without a pole or a top five. In 1999, he managed only one top 10, a fifth place at New Hampshire in the summer, and stumbled to 21st in points—just about off the chart.

Bill Elliott

Then the bombshell dropped. Word began to spread in April 1999 that McDonald's would leave the team after 2000. McDonald's issued a denial. Then, two weeks later at California, company officials confirmed the rumors to Bill on Friday and made public their plans to leave the next day.

"We honest to God did not have a clue it was coming," Elliott remembers. "They came in and said, 'We're getting ready to leave, and oh, by the way, we're going to have a Winston Cup deal in 2001.'

"It wasn't very good. It just added to what the hell else can happen."

McDonald's planned to run a Busch team with new owner Cal Wells in 2000, then step back up to Winston Cup with Wells in 2001. Wells also had acquired Winston Cup sponsorship from Tide, then with Rudd, for 2000, for driver Scott Pruett.

Life got even better in 1996 with the birth of his son Chase (right). Bill was a much happier person and it showed (below)!

Elliott was realist enough to know that odds were long in trying to find new sponsorship and keep the team going.

"It gets discouraging," he says. "This business is so much what you do today, what are you going to do tomorrow. A lot of these guys are quick to throw you in the creek—'you're too old, too this, too that'—and it isn't like that. If you get the right stuff, the right deal, anybody can win races.

"I had to weigh the whole thing out. Here I'm looking at McDonald's leaving. Owner-drivers are like the plague nowadays as far as going into the sponsors, the day of that stuff is gone. If you don't find the right deal to do, you might as well just quit. There's no reason just to ride around and make laps.

Bill's wife Cindy has been a big reason for his rejuvenated spirit and attitude. Her devotion to Bill and his image has been far more visible than most wives'. Below, Bill leads his old ride, The Melling T-Bird.

"The problem too is that if your guys get wind you're losing the sponsor, they're gone just like that. They don't know where the stability is."

Robert Yates, who was planning to replace driver Kenny Irwin, approached Bill shortly afterward about driving his number 28, but the timing was wrong. Elliott still believed he could find some way to keep his group together. "There were too many things in place, and I couldn't just walk away," Bill says. Rudd instead was hired to drive the Texaco car.

By September, the game was about over, and Elliott had to admit it. What saved the day came out of the blue—or rather, out of the red, the red of a new Winston Cup effort from Dodge. Dodge had lured away Ray Evernham, championship crew chief with Jeff Gor-

25 Years and Still on Fire

Bill learned in early 1999 that McDonalds would no longer support him after the year 2000. After an unsuccessful intense search for new sponsorship for his owner/driver team, Bill was faced with a decision that would be career and family impacting, thus leaving approximately 40 families without income. Bill opted to join Ray Evernham in the creation of a newly formed racing team that would utilize Bill's existing team and also bring back DaimlerChrysler into a new era of Winston Cup Racing. Bill will be driving the #9 Dodge Intrepid owned by Evernham Motorsports and sponsored by DaimlerChrysler in the year 2001.

The fall race at Martinsville gave Bill an opportunity to show his new teammate, Casey Atwood #19, a few pointers. Bill's new Boss, Ray Evernham, chose the experienced Bill Elliott to be a mentor for the young rookie. Bill's team has managed to help put the car on the pole at Charlotte (right) more than once with their quick pit work and his nimble driving.

don, designated him owner of the brand's two-car factory team for 2001, and gave him the resources to go find the best. Evernham's stated aim was to pair a popular veteran star with a young driver. The veteran star he chose was Bill Elliott.

"Ray came to me at Loudon [New Hampshire] last fall and said, 'If I did a race team, would you drive the car?'" Bill remembers. "I was like, my mouth dropped open, and I didn't say anything because I was too dumbfounded. My comment was I'd love to but there's a lot of things I'd have to work out.

"I wanted to try to get to a point and try to look at sponsorship, but I still look back on it, and if I'd re-upped with McDonald's when Cal Wells did, it isn't enough money. Today I look at that and say, 'Whew, I'm glad I didn't do that deal because at the end of the day, it wouldn't be enough.' Really, everything happened for the best from the standpoint of timing."

Plans were made for Evernham to acquire Elliott's Statesville assets. In March 2000 at Atlanta, Bill Elliott was announced as driver for Dodge Motorsports.

Next year, Elliott will be teamed up with 20-year-old Casey Atwood, who has raced the past two seasons in the Busch Series. Courtesy of the Melling team, which also is changing to Dodge, Elliott again will drive number 9, with Atwood in number 19.

With Dodge's resources and Evernham's progressive guidance, Bill had crept back toward the top 15 in points and generally looked competitive again, starting the season with third place in the 2000 Daytona 500. He ran dependably top 10 through spring and summer, with third in the Brickyard 400 at Indianapolis, before misfortune sidetracked him. Elliott

broke his left kneecap in August and missed the races at Bristol and Darlington. But he was back in the hunt at Richmond.

In 2001, McDonald's and Ford, two long-time Elliott icons, will be gone, and Bill will be driving the red, factory-backed Dodge. *A Dodge.* Even after a year of talk, that shocked many, given the family's 60-year heritage with Ford and career-long loyalty to the make.

Nothing stays the same in racing.

"When you get down to May, June, July, if you haven't got something [sponsorship] nailed down by July . . ." Bill explains. "You might luck into something, but when November comes and the last payment comes, you've got some serious questions to ask yourself. I'm not a Felix, not a Hendrick, not a Roush. I don't have other ways to subsidize this deal. And with the amount of money you're spending day-in, day-out, there ain't no way in heck you can compete.

"I just looked at the options, what it was going to cost to run the deal, what other teams were available, what other options were available—not just for me but for the whole entity. It's the one that made the most sense.

Lately, Bill's career has seen its ups and downs. A big downer has been several injuries (right). But Bill has still managed to make it to victory lane a few times. Bill also won Daytona's 125 Qualifier (above).

Bill Elliott

"It's disappointing from one aspect, but it's encouraging in another. It isn't like at the end of the year you shut the doors and your people don't have work. Now you're working toward a goal. We'll have all our people organized, and they know where their future is. To me that says a lot. It's relieved me because I know where everybody's staying."

Elliott says he'll still be the same Bill.

"After our announcement, the first Ford fan appreciation day we went to, I was literally scared to death," he says. "Up on the stage, I was totally amazed. I was pleasantly surprised at the understanding the people had of the position I and this race team were in.

"It gets back to the David-and-Goliath deal. We're fighting multi-car teams, a lot more money, a lot more resources. I feel like we've done a good job at it, my family and what we have fought through in the last 15 years. To be able to come here and still be halfway competitive at the end of the day . . ."

Bill's Trusty Steeds

Bill has always had a livery full of
equipment that fills his need for speed,
from motorcycles to airplanes and
helicopters. But his real workhorses
have been his race cars. This section
is devoted to those race cars.

At Darlington in 1977 (middle) Bill ran with Jimmy Means's number 52. Shortly afterward, he moved into a Mercury (above) and a color
change to red, which has been the dominant color ever since. When Bill ran his first Winston Cup race at Rockingham, it was in a blue Ford
Torino, which carried the number 9 that he used on local tracks (top).

After that, it was back into his Mercury. Melling came on board the red Mercury briefly in 1980. In 1982, it became a fixture for the entire season, and the car changed to a Ford Thunderbird. The boxy T-Bird ran mostly red but did run a few races in blue paint (right). In 1983, the T-Bird became more aerodynamic (bottom).

Coor's replaced the Melling name in 1984, and their backing helped Bill win three races that year. The next year, 1985, Bill drove this car to surprise victory in the Daytona 500 and won 10 more races that year. In those days NASCAR allowed chrome wheels.

The Coors T-Bird (left), carried Bill to the 1988 Winston Cup Championship over the reigning champ, Dale Earnhardt. Earnhardt, who became "The Man in Black" in 1988, had been the champ the previous two years. The car below won over a million dollars for Bill at Darlington.

Ford gave T-Bird a new look for 1989 (top), and Coors gave Bill a new color in 1991. It was to be their last year with Bill.

Running a few local short tracks as well as NASCAR Busch Grand National races has afforded Bill the opportunity to try on a variety of hats and cars. Here are a few he's tried: the Ford Falcon (top left), a modified Mustang (above), a Pontiac (bottom left), and a Buick (below).

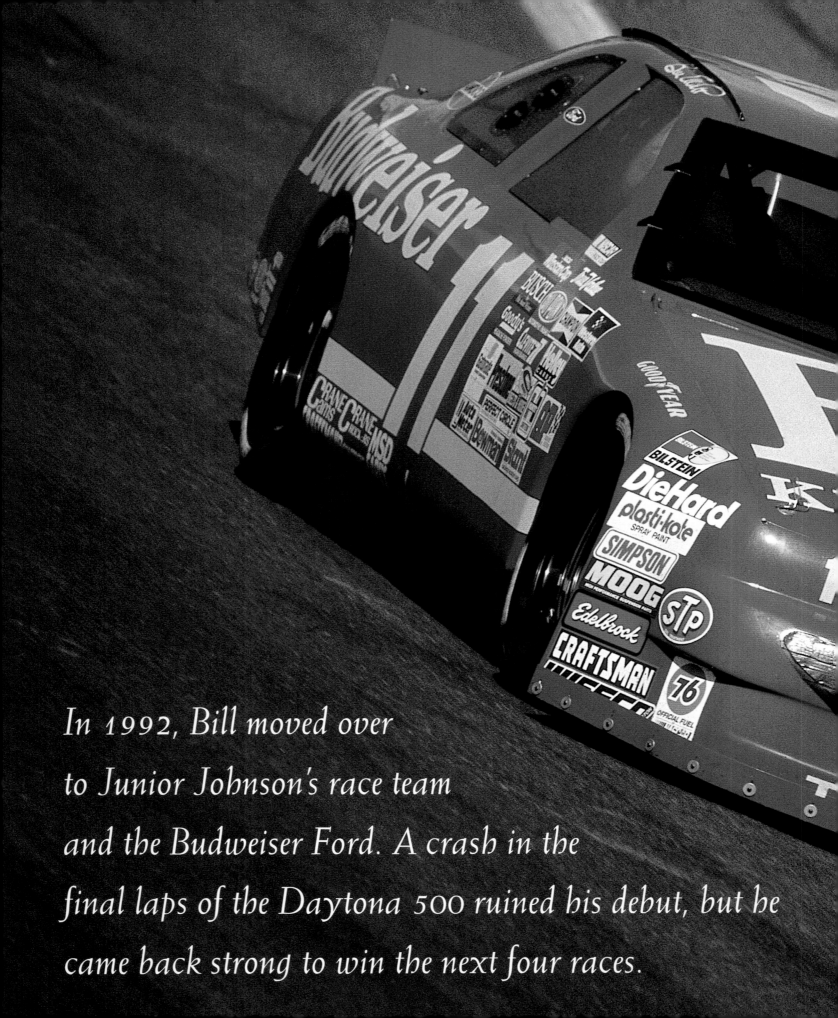

In 1992, Bill moved over
to Junior Johnson's race team
and the Budweiser Ford. A crash in the
final laps of the Daytona 500 ruined his debut, but he
came back strong to win the next four races.

When McDonald's decided they wanted to back the "Most Popular Driver," they went with Bill Elliott in 1995. Still Ford, still red, but now with a new number in memory of his brother Ernie's son, Casey Elliott, number 94.

With NASCAR's "Most Popular Driver" as its spokesperson, McDonald's saw a "golden" opportunity to use Bill's car as a means to enhance its product and promotional tie-ins. (above) In a first-of-its-kind joint promotion with McDonald's and Warner Brothers Studios, Bill unveiled the "Thunderbat" in 1995. (opposite page) Three other on-track promotions included (top) a colorful tie-dye design scheme to "get back with Big Mac"; (center) a standout gold car to honor NASCAR's 50th Anniversary in 1998; (bottom) a midnight blue shade for the "Mac Tonight" campaign.

After 25 years of racing in NASCAR's premier division,
Bill is still fired up and charging ahead
with his new team.

BILL ELLIOTT—

Fan Friendly, Fan Favorite

Perhaps as awesome as Elliott's achievements on the race track—the speed records, the championship, the Winston Million—is a singular honor off the track—his 15 (and counting) Most Popular Driver awards, presented by the National Motorsports Press Association and awarded by the fans.

With the exception of two seasons, 1989 and 1990, Bill has earned the tribute every year since 1984. That, of course, includes seasons when he was king of the hill and seasons when up looked a long way off.

The 1999 award was the 14th presented, the first going to Curtis Turner in 1956. With 14, that means Bill Elliott has won nearly a third of all the most-popular awards ever presented. No one—not Richard Petty, not Bobby Allison—is anywhere close.

The reason for this fantastic run is Bill's loyal legion of fans, and there are no fans like Elliott fans. Their allegiance and affection transcend the success or failure of their hero. The Bill Elliott Fan Club, up to 7,000 single members strong, annually gets out the vote with an organized campaign via letter, phone, and now web site.

The shrine of Elliott fans is, naturally, the Elliott Museum on the family racing complex in Dawsonville, which will be moving to Thunder Road USA in the summer of 2001. On display are cars, trophies, plaques, and photographs commemorating the highs and lows of 30-plus years in racing.

More impressive, however, are countless items, ranging from quilts to children's drawings to carefully crafted scale-size tableaux, showing, for instance, a pit stop. Some of these memorabilia obviously took days to produce, then were sent respectfully to the museum. Fan mail is filed in dozens of binders, and Museum directors Kathy Peterson and Dixie Price, Fan Club President, say much more of same just cannot be displayed.

Peterson and Price say they have seen first-time pilgrims kneel and kiss the floor upon arriving inside the Museum. They say they hear countless stories about children named Chase, after Bill's son, Dawson, after Dawsonville—or even pets named Awesome Bill. The tales of devotion go on and on.

Right: Bill has been involved with MAKE-A-WISH Foundation for many years. This foundation strives to grant wishes to children and young people under the age of twenty-one with life-threatening illnesses. Here Amanda Zimmerman (beside Bill) and her sister Ashley, pose with Bill at Atlanta Motor Speedway in November 1999. Amanda's dreams came true, being able to tell her favorite driver to "Start Your Engine" before the start of the race.

Bill Elliott

Early in his career, Bill showed a fine appreciation for his fans. With the stands empty and other drivers on their way home, Bill will often be found meeting his admirers.

Some testimonials, from the true believers:

Bill,

My name is Michael Stone. I am 10 years old and live in Richmond, Va. I try to go to all your autograph sessions that we can, but I see you the most at Martinsville. I am in your fan club and race go-karts at Amelia Motor Raceway. This is my first year and right now I am in 4th place in the points. I know that one day if I keep racing my go-kart and move up thru the lower classes of NASCAR that I can be a Winston Cup driver just like you. You are my hero.

PS Here are some pictures of my bedroom and my go-kart.

* * *

Bill—

I've been a fan of yours going on 10 years now. My dad has been a NASCAR fan for as long as I can remember, and being a "Daddy's Girl" I enjoy NASCAR as much as he does. He's always backed that black #3, while I rooted for the red #9, blue #9, red #11, and the #94, no matter what color it is.

I just want you to know there are a lot of faithful Bill Elliott fans out there, like myself, backing you a full 110%. You are the BEST!

Your #1 fan in the World

Melissa Harrod

* * *

Bill Elliott

Dear Mr. Elliott,

My temporary fan club certificate arrived and I was so excited. The weeks we can't make it to the track, we are glued to the TV. We saw the interview with you and Ray Evernham. Needless to say, we are thrilled that this will be a good career move for you but are also "dyed in the wool" Ford people. It will be a time of mixed emotions for us, as it will be for you, but I have to be loyal to the driver and give Dodge a chance. May God bless you.

Carol S. Crow

* * *

Dear Bill,

We want you to know that we know you are doing all you can do and that we are behind you 100%! We realize that many, many things are beyond your control, and for this reason we are enclosing a 4-leaf clover for you—maybe it can help offset some of the troubles others around you have and are affecting you. We wish you all the luck and look forward to hearing about your new plans and opportunities. We believe in you and know you will overcome all of this and you are the better person and will continue to be. We have the faith and will keep the faith.

Delisa and Jeff Smith

* * *

It's not unusual to see some drivers avoid the crowds. You can watch a driver stay as far away from the fence as possible, walk down the middle of pit road, or pretend to be engaged in deep conversation with a crew member, but not Bill. He'll walk right up to his fans and give them all the time he can spare.

ALWAYS ACCOMMODATING

Bill will not shy away from personal appearances. Few drivers will be as busy as Bill. Newspapers will carry notices of Bill meeting fans at the local McDonald's, a Ford dealer, at his shop in Statesville, North Carolina, or his museum in Georgia. The man is in demand!

Bill Elliott

FANS RETURN THE FAVOR

Fans will stand in long lines for hours just to meet Bill (below). When they do get to see him, they will ask for autographs or photos, but many will want to leave a gift for him—some item to express their heartfelt feelings for Bill. It could be a giant card (above, left) with hundreds of signatures from his fan club members. Or an elaborate quilt (above, right) that is decorated with dozens of photos of Bill's career. A trip to his museum or shop will amaze the visitors with the many handmade items his fans send to show their appreciation.

Bill Elliott

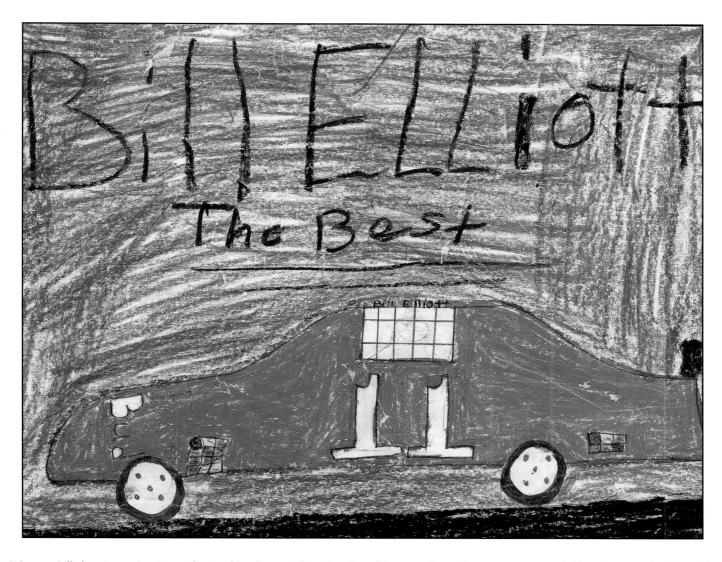

It is especially heartwarming to see the touching letters Bill receives from his young fans. Many are accompanied by photos or drawings. The next few pages include a very small sampling of the letters on display at the Elliott family museum.

BILL ELLIOTT IS THE BEST

Why BILL ELLIOTT is my favorite winston cup driver

 I watch BILL ELLIOTT every week a race is on + cheer him on.
He tries hard + is nice to his fans. I met him in Daytona.
 I collect all his stuff + we have the same NAME. In 10
years I want to drive just like Bill. He is my

          H   E   R   O.

By Elliott Streader   Age 8
 562 N.W. 46 Street
Boca Raton, Florida 33431
 (407)368 0250

P.S. His wife is pretty to.

RECEIVED
OCT 1 9 1993

HAPPY BIRTHDAY BILL ELLIOTT

It can be a long wait, but it is worth it, to get a chance to talk with Bill, take pictures and get an autograph. The food and entertainment are always great, too!

Bill will do just about anything his fans ask him to do. That includes not only signing autographs, but even signing cars.

Bill Elliott

Marry Christmas Mr. Bill Elliott

Dear Mr. Elliott,

Hi my name is Michael Miller I'm ten years old. You are favorite Driver. The reason that I'm sending you this pictur is that I don't have any money. I went to Atlanta To see the race I'm looking forward to next year.

Your Fan,
Michael Miller

by : Michael Miller of 400 North Church St. Woodstock Va.

WHY BILL ELLIOTT IS MY FAVORITE WINSTON CUP DRIVER

Bill always takes the time out of his busy schedule to devote a bonding relationship with everyone. His smile, warmth and personality makes Bill #1 all the way around. I use his warmth as a Role Model for my life. Bill will always be my Favorite Winston Cup Driver.

Michelle Johnson
Route 2, Box 249
Pageland, SC   29728
Age: 11

Michelle Johnson

Bill Elliott   153

A FUN DAY...

A fan visiting Bill's shop on his special open house days will have a lot to do. Not only do they get to tour the shop, but loads of activities are available for kids and their parents. Check out these photos and you can see games like bingo, darts, musical chairs, and slot car racing. You can also get balloons, prizes, or photos with Bill or the race car.

...AT BILL'S PLACE

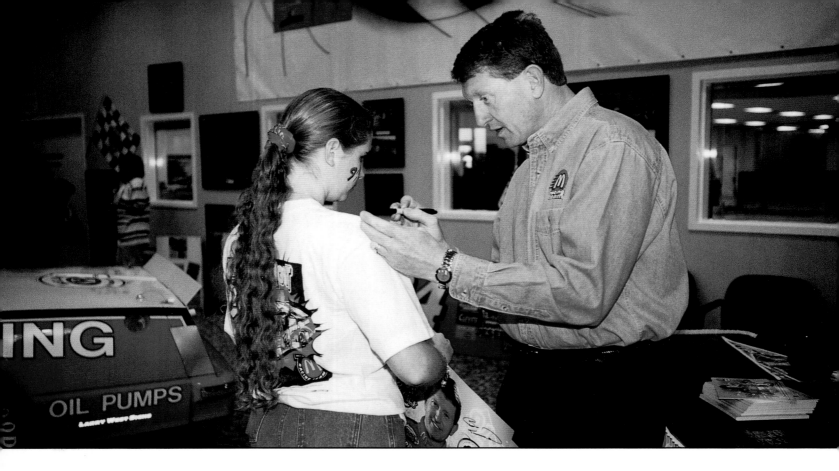

Bill's sterling reputation and friendly manner draws the affection of children. Any gathering for Bill will have almost as many children as adults.

Bill Elliott

Dear Bill Elliott Fan Club,

My name is Cassi M. Hartsell. My family and I are in your fan club. I am 11 years old. I am entering my essay on "Why Bill Elliott is My Favorite Winston Cup Driver." He's my favorite driver because he never crashes anybody, he tries his best to win or finish in the top ten, he is a nice guy, he is a totally awesome driver, he is a winner no matter if he wins or not, he's the best Winston Cup driver I have ever seen, he's my idol.

That's my essay on "Why Bill Elliott is my favorite Winston Cup driver.

Your Best Fans,

Cassi Hartsell & Family

Above: Brittany and Chase Elliott prepare for the festivities at the Moonshine Festival in Dawsonville in October 2000.

Elliott Year-By-Year Record

Year	Races	Won	2nd	3rd	4th	5th	6-10	DNF	Poles	Money Won	Point Standing
1976	8	0	0	0	0	0	0	6	0	$ 11,635	41
1977	10	0	0	0	0	0	2	5	0	20,575	35
1978	10	0	0	0	0	0	5	3	0	42,065	33
1979	13	0	1	0	0	0	4	2	0	57,450	28
1980	11	0	0	0	0	0	4	4	0	42,545	34
1981	13	0	0	0	1	0	6	5	1	70,320	30
1982	21	0	3	3	1	1	1	6	1	226,780	25
1983	30	1	4	1	3	3	10	4	0	479,965	3
1984	30	3	1	4	4	1	11	2	4	660,226	3
1985	28	11	2	0	2	1	2	3	11	2,433,187	2
1986	29	2	0	2	1	3	8	6	4	1,069,142	4
1987	29	6	3	1	5	1	4	5	8	1,619,210	2
1988	29	6	2	2	4	1	7	1	6	1,574,639	1
1989	29	3	0	1	3	1	6	4	2	854,570	6
1990	29	1	4	1	5	1	4	2	2	1,090,730	4
1991	29	1	2	1	0	2	6	2	2	705,605	11
1992	29	5	2	3	1	3	3	2	2	1,692,381	2
1993	30	0	1	2	2	1	9	3	2	955,859	8
1994	31	1	1	3	0	1	6	5	1	936,779	10
1995	31	0	0	0	2	2	6	4	2	996,816	8
1996	24	0	0	0	0	0	6	2	0	716,506	30
1997	32	0	1	0	3	1	9	3	1	1,607,827	8
1998	32	0	0	0	0	0	5	7	0	1,618,421	18
1999	34	0	0	0	0	1	1	4	0	1,624,101	21
2000	32	0	0	2	1	0	4	8	0	2,580,823	21
Totals	**623**	**40**	**27**	**26**	**38**	**24**	**129**	**98**	**49**	**$23,688,157***	

*Includes post-season bonus money and the Winston Million [1985]. Car Owners: Elliott Family, 1976-81; Harry Melling, 1982-91; Junior Johnson, 1992-94; Bill Elliott/Charles Hardy, 1995-96**; Bill Elliott, 1997-99
**Eliott became sole owner of team in July, 1996.

Elliott Winston Cup Wins-By-Year

1983
Riverside [#2]

1984
Michigan [#1]
Charlotte [#2]
Rockingham [#2]

1985
Daytona 500 [#1]
Darlington [#1]
Atlanta [#1]
Talladega [#1]
Dover [#1]
Pocono [#1]
Michigan [#1]
Pocono [#2]
Michigan [#2]
Darlington [#2]
Atlanta [#2]

1986
Michigan [#1]
Michigan [#2]

1987
Daytona 500 [#1]
Talladega [#2]
Michigan [#2]
Charlotte [#2]
Rockingham [#2]
Atlanta [#2]

1988
Bristol [#1]
Dover [#1]
Daytona [#2]
Pocono [#2]
Darlington [#2]
Dover [#2]

1989
Michigan [#1]
Pocono [#2]
Phoenix

1990
Dover [#2]

1991
Daytona [#2]

1992
Rockingham [#1]
Richmond [#1]
Atlanta [#1]
Darlington [#1]
Atlanta [#2]

1994
Darlington [#2]

Elliott Winston Cup Wins-By-Track

Atlanta [5 wins]
1985 [#1 & #2]
1987 [#2]
1992 [#1 & #2]

Bristol [1 win]
1988 [#1]

Charlotte [2 wins]
1984 [#2]
1987 [#2]

Darlington [5 wins]
1985 [#1 & #2]
1988 [#2]
1992 [#1]
1994 [#2]

Daytona [4 wins]
1985 [#1-500]
1987 [#1-500]
1988 [#2]
1991 [#2]

Dover [4 wins]
1985 [#1]
1988 [#1 & #2]
1990 [#2]

Michigan [7 wins]
1984 [#1]
1985 [#1 & #2]
1986 [#1 & #2]
1987 [#2]
1989 [#1]

Phoenix [1 win]
1989

Pocono [4 wins]
1985 [#1 & #2]
1988 [#2]
1989 [#2]

Richmond [1 win]
1992 [#1]

Riverside* [1 win]
1983 [#2]

Rockingham [3 wins]
1984 [#2]
1987 [#2]
1992 [#1]

Talladega [2 wins]
1985 [#1]
1987 [#2]

*inactive

Autographs